ESSENTIAL SPIRITUAL WARFARE PRAYERS

ESSENTIAL SPIRITUAL WARFARE PRAYERS

FOR PROTECTION AND DELIVERANCE

Written and compiled by

Mary Leonora Wilson, FSP

Pauline

BOOKS & MEDIA

Boston

Nihil Obstat: Reverend James R. Mattaliano, S.J., M. Div., M.Th.
Imprimatur: ✠ Seán Cardinal O'Malley, O.F.M. Cap.
    Archbishop of Boston
    December 21, 2020

ISBN 10: 0-8198-2412-7
ISBN 13: 978-0-8198-2412-7

Cover design by Danielle Victoria Lussier, FSP

Published by Pauline Books & Media, 50 Saint Pauls Avenue, Boston, MA 02130-3491

Printed in the U.S.A.

www.pauline.org

Pauline Books & Media is the publishing house of the Daughters of St. Paul, an international congregation of women religious serving the Church with the communications media.

1 2 3 4 5 6 7 8 9   25 24 23 22 21

Contents

I.

THE SACRAMENTS:
POWERFUL DEFENSES AGAINST EVIL

II.

GOD'S WORD

III.

BASIC PRAYERS

IV.

PRAYERS TO JESUS OUR LORD AND REDEEMER

V.

PRAYERS TO GOD THE HOLY SPIRIT

VI.

PRAYERS TO THE MOST BLESSED VIRGIN MARY

VII.

Prayers to Saint Joseph, Guardian of the Holy Family and Terror of Demons

VIII.

Prayers to the Angels for Protection

IX.

PRAYERS TO THE SAINTS
for HELP AND PROTECTION

X.

SPIRITUAL WARFARE PRAYERS

Foreword

The spiritual battle of humanity goes all the way back to the Garden of Eden. In Genesis 3:15 we read that God will put enmity between the serpent and the woman, between its offspring and hers; "He will strike at your head, while you strike at his heel."

In the Book of Revelation 12:7–9 we hear of Satan being thrown down to earth along with the other fallen angels (now demons) where, filled with rage, he wages war against the rest of the offspring of the woman clothed with the sun, and with her Son.

This is the world and the reality in which we live, but as Christians, we are not to fear or be disheartened. Jesus has promised us that he has overcome the world (Jn 16:33).

All of us are called to take courage and to choose whom we will serve. A choice for the

Lord will always leave us open for attack from the enemy of creation.

The attacks made upon us are ultimately further attacks on God as Satan rages against him and all that is holy, true, and divine. Satan has eternally and permanently lost, yet he wishes to take as many souls down with him as possible, as he continues to sweep his tail in an attempt to cast the star of our lives into the darkness of his separation (see Rv 12:1–4).

To withstand Satan's assault upon our souls, we must arm ourselves with the weapons of faith (Eph 6) and use the means available to us that guarantee our ultimate victory: prayer, fasting, sacrifice, regular confession, Mass, the Eucharist, Adoration, the Rosary, the Scapular, Sacred Scripture, and the use of sacramentals (the Chaplets of Divine Mercy and of Saint Michael, the Saint Benedict and Miraculous Medals, holy water, etc.). In using these effective means, we prevent the enemy from robbing us of our true destiny—union with God.

Jesus reminds us that apart from him we can do nothing but, trusting in him, his abiding presence and saving power are with us (see Jn 15:4–7).

The Apostle James exhorts us to submit to God and resist the devil, who will flee from us (Jas 5:7). This submitting to God is all about fostering, developing, and deepening a relationship with him through prayer and the spiritual life. We must remain very close to Jesus, Mary, Saint Joseph (the "Terror of Demons"), Saint Michael, all the angels, and the saints. In doing so we arm ourselves against the assaults of the enemy that assuredly come to us. May these prayers bring you the protection and deliverance the Lord desires for you and your loved ones.

JAMES R. MATTALIANO, S.J.

President of the Pope Leo XIII Institute (For the education and training of priests in the holy ministry of exorcism and deliverance)

Introduction
Jesus, the Source of Our Faith

"I do not ask that you take them out of the world but that you keep them from the evil one" (Jesus' prayer to the Father for his disciples the night before he died, Jn 17:15).

When Jesus and the three apostles with him descended from the mount of the transfiguration, they were met by a crowd of people and a distraught father, who had brought his son to the disciples that they might rid him of a spirit that was tormenting him. The disciples had been unable to cast the spirit out of the boy. Almost as a last resort, the father turns to Jesus and cries: "'If you can do anything, have compassion on us and help us.' Jesus said to him, 'If you can! Everything is possible to one who has faith.'

Then the boy's father cried out, 'I do believe, help my unbelief!' Jesus, on seeing a crowd rapidly gathering, rebuked the unclean spirit and said to it, 'Mute and deaf spirit, I command you: come out of him and never enter him again!' Shouting and throwing the boy into convulsions, it came out" (Mk 9:22–26). The disciples were as amazed as everyone else. Later, in private, they asked Jesus, "Why could we not drive it out?" Two answers are recorded, both important to the topic of this booklet. Matthew remembers Jesus answering: "Because of your little faith. Amen, I say to you, if you have faith the size of a mustard seed, you will say to this mountain, 'Move from here to there,' and it will move. Nothing will be impossible for you" (Mt 17:20). And Mark records these words of the Master: "This kind can only come out through prayer" (Mk 9:29).

Faith and prayer are two very powerful weapons that God has equipped us with in the battle against evil. It is Jesus himself who teaches us, by example, by encouragement, and even by admonition, to pray to be delivered from evil. Jesus prays and fasts for forty days and forty nights in the desert before his encounter with Satan. He prays nights and in the early morning hours before driving out demons and healing and teaching. He prepares for his passion in intense and profound prayer and urges his disciples to do the same: "Watch and pray that you may not undergo the test. The spirit is willing, but the flesh is weak" (Mk 14:38). In teaching us how to pray to the Father, Jesus includes these very important words: "do not subject us to the final test but deliver us from the evil one" (Mt 6:13).

The *Catechism of the Catholic Church* reminds us that this last petition of the Our Father is not dealing with abstracts, but is referring to a real person, Satan, the leader of those angels who opposed God before the creation of the world and who even sought to ruin the plan of redemption accomplished in Jesus (see *CCC* 2851). Saint Paul is also explicit: "Our struggle is not with flesh and blood but with the principalities, with the powers, with the world rulers of this present darkness, with the evil spirits in the heavens" (Eph 6:12).

All of Scripture speaks of the need of spiritual warfare against the spirits of evil. Should we be afraid or anxious? Not at all. God permits Satan to exercise power over the natural world and lets him tempt us, but he will not be victorious in the end. Saint Paul says, "If God is for us, who can be against us?" (Rom 8:31). In everything "we conquer overwhelmingly through him who loved us. For I am convinced that neither death, nor life, nor angels, nor principalities, nor present things, nor future things, nor powers, nor height, nor depth, nor any other creature will be able to separate us from the love of God in Christ Jesus our Lord" (Rom 8:37–39).

Jesus our Redeemer is the source of our faith; he marches ahead of us, alongside us, with us. If we do not abandon him, he will not abandon us. It is he who assures us of victory, and because of him we can fight bravely and confidently: "Behold, I am with you always, until the end of the age" (Mt 28:20).

I

The Sacraments

Powerful Defenses Against Evil

It's important to recognize the forces of evil in the world so that we can be prepared to resist them. We are not called to be exorcists. Major exorcisms (i.e., expulsion of demons and/or liberation from demonic possession) can be performed only by a priest with the permission of a bishop (see *CCC* 1673). But we can protect and defend ourselves from demonic activity by avoiding sin and renouncing sinful habits; by deepening our relationship with the Lord through prayer, Scripture, and the sacraments; by deepening our knowledge of the faith and living a life of virtue—especially the virtues of humility, charity, and dependence upon God; by seeking the support of Mary, the angels, and the saints; and by making use of the sacramentals provided by the Church.

In the Book of Genesis, we read the story of God's rejection of Cain's offering and how angry Cain was. God then speaks to Cain: "Why are you angry . . . ? If you do well, will you not be accepted? And if you do not do well, sin is lurking at the door; its desire is for you, but you must master it" (Gn 4:6–7). In our struggle against the powers of darkness, sin is the evil, Satan is the instigator of sin.

Have you ever experienced sin lurking at your door? Perhaps in your thoughts or in your heart? Saint Paul did. He writes to the Romans: "When I want to do right, evil is at hand. For I take delight in the law of God, in my inner self, but I see in my members another principle at war with the law of my mind, taking me captive to the law of sin that dwells in my members" (Rom 7:21–23). Isn't this often our own experience? Sin lurking at the door . . . "Miserable one that I am! Who will deliver me from this mortal body? Thanks be to God through Jesus Christ our Lord" (Rom 7:24–25).

The first means of defense against Satan is to recognize sin lurking at our door, to call it by name, to avoid it, and to renounce sinful habits. This is possible through the grace won for us through the passion and death of Jesus Christ and poured into our hearts by the Holy Spirit in Baptism, in Confirmation, and in the sacraments of Eucharist and Reconciliation. The sacraments are there for us, to strengthen us and to draw us into a deeper relationship with Jesus Christ. With his grace we become formidable against the enemy. In his first letter to the Corinthians, Paul reminds us, "God is faithful and will not let you be tried beyond your strength; but with the trial he will also provide a way out, so that you may be able to bear it" (1 Cor 10:13).

One very effective way to prepare ourselves for trials and spiritual combat is a sacramental life: frequent confession, frequent Communion, and at least weekly participation at Sunday Mass. If daily Mass is a possibility, even better. The more we nourish ourselves with the Eucharist, the better prepared we will be. In the sacraments given us by Jesus we have an arsenal and an invaluable source of grace!

Regularly renewing our baptismal vows and affirming our faith in the creed of the Church are important spiritual practices that strengthen us in our Christian identity, by constantly reminding us whose we are.

Baptism

Renewal of Baptismal Promises

V. Do you renounce Satan?
R. I do.

V. And all his works?
R. I do.

V. And all his empty promises?
R. I do.

V. Do you believe in God, the Father almighty, Creator of heaven and earth?
R. I do.

V. Do you believe in Jesus Christ, his only Son, our Lord, who was born of the Virgin Mary, suffered death and was buried, rose again from the dead, and is seated at the right hand of the Father?
R. I do.

V. Do you believe in the Holy Spirit, the holy Catholic Church, the communion of saints, the forgiveness of sins, the resurrection of the body, and life everlasting?

R. I do.

And may almighty God, the Father of our Lord Jesus Christ, who has given us a new birth by water and the Holy Spirit, and bestowed on us the forgiveness of our sins, keep us by his grace, in Christ Jesus our Lord, for eternal life. Amen.

Eucharist

Act of Love before Communion

Jesus Master, you assure me: "I am the Life," and "whoever eats my flesh and drinks my blood will have eternal life." In Baptism and in the sacrament of Reconciliation you have communicated to me this life of yours. Now you nourish it by making yourself my food. Take my heart; detach it from the vain things of the world. I love you with all my heart, above all things, because you are the supreme good and my eternal happiness.

Prayer of Saint Thomas Aquinas after Communion

I give you thanks, Lord, holy Father, almighty and eternal God, who have been pleased to nourish me, a sinner and your unworthy servant, with the precious Body and Blood of your Son, our Lord Jesus Christ: this through no merits of mine, but due solely to the graciousness of your mercy.

And I pray that this Holy Communion may not be for me an offense to be punished, but a saving plea for forgiveness. May it be for me the armor of faith, and the shield of good will. May it cancel my faults; destroy concupiscence and carnal passion; increase charity and patience, humility and obedience and all the virtues. May it be a firm defense against the snares of all my enemies, both visible and invisible, the complete calming of my impulses, both of the flesh and of the spirit, a firm adherence to you, the one true God, and the joyful completion of my life's course.

And I beseech you to lead me, a sinner, to that banquet beyond all telling, where with your Son and the Holy Spirit you are the true light of your saints, fullness of satisfied desire, eternal gladness, consummate delight, and perfect happiness. Through Christ our Lord. Amen.

Spiritual Communion

My Jesus, I believe that you are present in the Blessed Sacrament. I love you above everything, and I long for you in my soul. Since I cannot now receive you sacramentally, come at least spiritually into my heart. I embrace you as if you were already there and unite myself entirely to you; do not allow me to be separated from you.

Reconciliation

In the sacrament of Reconciliation (also called Penance or confession), we present ourselves contrite before God, who showers his healing grace on our souls. Through this sacrament, God repairs and strengthens our baptismal bonds both with himself and with the Church. Confession brings us to Christ, who fills us with life. Because going to confession can powerfully change us, it's the last thing the devil wants. So we can expect many barriers and obstacles and much emotional resistance to the sacrament. We should go anyway. Jesus wants to meet us in this sacrament and fill us with life so that we may be strengthened against the temptations of Satan and prepared for death and judgment.

How to Make a Good Confession

1. Decide to go to confession at a regular time weekly, monthly, or as frequently as needed, and stick with this resolution.

2. Before confession, reflect and ask the Holy Spirit for the grace to understand clearly how your behavior has damaged your

relationship with God, the Church, and persons in your life.

3. Begin with a Sign of the Cross and tell the priest how long it has been since your last confession.

4. Tell the priest your sins. Be as straightforward as you can; don't make excuses.

5. Listen for any words from the priest that may help you deepen your faithfulness to Christ and avoid repeating the sins. (If the priest is unhelpful, don't worry; the grace of the sacrament is the reason you are there. God's grace is always efficacious.)

6. When the priest gives you a penance, indicate that you understand it, or ask for clarification if you don't.

7. Say an Act of Contrition.

8. Listen to the words of absolution.

9. Take some time in prayer to complete your penance or do it as soon as possible if the penance is an act of charity.

10. Thank God for this great moment of grace in your life.

Prayer Before Confession

Lord, I kneel here before you and ask you to clear my mind of all distraction so I can spend this time preparing to receive this sacrament of love, healing, and forgiveness. Help me to see how I have offended you and my neighbor. Take away anything that would blur my inner vision so I can confess my sins with a sincere mind and heart. Remove any fears that might prevent truthfulness, and allow peace and trust to enter my being.

Examination of Conscience

An important part of preparing for the sacrament of Reconciliation is an examination of conscience. During this exercise, the penitent sets time aside to think and to pray. The main question to ask ourselves is: How well have I been living as a disciple of Jesus Christ, and where have I failed?

Sometimes we can answer this question immediately. There will be obvious examples of failure. Each of us has long-established patterns of weakness. We find ourselves making the same mistakes and committing the same sins repeatedly, the "old standbys" that keep us awake at night. But there are also more subtle ways in which we stray from Christ's example. Sin hides well. By looking at ourselves carefully, though, we may discover the unexpected sins in our lives. We may even be able to see patterns of sin that we did not recognize before. Clarity is the purpose of examining one's conscience. By seeing more clearly, we are better able to seek the help we need. By seeking help, we become freer in drawing closer to God.

As you prepare for confession, ask God to help you see and accept the particular sins for which you are responsible. Then explore your behavior since your last confession. One way to jog your mind and heart is through reflection on the Ten Commandments, which helps you focus your thoughts and look over your life.

In examining yourself, keep in mind that a thought not consented to, or an emotion felt but not followed through on, is not a sin. A sin is a thought, word, or deed that is objectively wrong, that you know is wrong, and that you do anyway; it can also be an omission— something you did not do, but knew you should do.

I am the Lord your God; you shall not have strange gods before me.

Have I loved something or someone more than God? Do I doubt God's love for me? Have I boasted about sinning? Have I let love of material goods, physical pleasures, or personal status determine my choices? Am I angry with God? Do I believe I don't need God? Have I denied the existence of God? Do I pray regularly? Have I broken vows or promises made to God? Have I been involved in the occult or sought control over my life through superstition, magic, witchcraft, or those who claim to possess psychic powers? Have I tried to grow in the knowledge of God through Scripture reading and prayer?

You shall not take the name of the Lord your God in vain.

Have I used the name of God as a curse or exclamation? Have I used the name of God, Jesus Christ, the Virgin Mary, or the saints with irreverence, hatred, or defiance? Have I belittled or spoken irreverently of the sacraments of the Church? Have I used vulgar or obscene language?

Have I used the name of God to coerce others to do my will? Have I sworn a false oath or lied while using God's name to prove my sincerity?

Remember the Sabbath day, to keep it holy.

Have I missed Mass on Sundays or holy days of obligation deliberately or through laziness? Have I knowingly received Holy Communion while in the state of mortal sin? Do I participate in the Christian community and bring support, encouragement, and strength to my parish? Do I make a time of rest for myself and those for whom I am responsible (e.g., family members, employees)? Do I avoid unnecessary work and shopping on Sundays?

Honor your father and your mother.

Have I shown due love, kindness, respect, and compassion to my parents? Am I willing to give encouragement and material assistance to my parents? Have I neglected their needs? Do I harbor resentments against my parents? Am I respectful of all family members? Have I educated my children in the faith? Do I show respect and due obedience to those in authority over me? Am I conscientious regarding my duties as a citizen? Do I support laws and public policies that strengthen the family?

You shall not kill.

Do I defend all human life at every stage? Have I taken the life of another, or unjustly inflicted bodily harm on another person? Have I participated in abortion, infanticide, or euthanasia? Have I encouraged or enabled another to do so or promoted laws that do so? Have I seriously considered or attempted suicide? Have I endangered the safety of others or myself through the abuse of alcohol or drugs, or through the irresponsible use of vehicles? Have I unlawfully sold or given drugs to another? Do I take reasonable care of my health? Have I held hatred for another person? Am I prejudiced or have I discriminated against anyone because of their race, color, nationality, sex, or religion? Do I respect the dignity of everyone? Have I willfully damaged the reputation of another? Have I ridiculed or insulted others? Have I bullied anyone or mercilessly teased them? Am I unable to control my anger? Have I been unforgiving or sought revenge? Do I delight in seeing others suffer? Have I been cruel or mean in words or deeds?

You shall not commit adultery. You shall not covet your neighbor's wife.

Have I engaged in sexual activity with someone other than my spouse? Do I respect the boundaries of relationships and the sanctity of marriage? Do I intentionally prevent the conception of children by artificial means? Do I accept the goodness of sexuality, for myself and others? Do I respect the needs of my spouse as regards the marital right? Do I accept the value of chastity for all unmarried persons? Have I willfully entertained impure thoughts or fantasies? Do I lust after the spouse of another? Do I nurse feelings of sexual desire for someone who is not my spouse? Do I use sexualized speech? Have I told or listened to impure jokes or music? Do I touch others or make gestures to satisfy sexual feelings? Have I purchased, viewed, or used pornography? Do I masturbate? Have I committed rape? Have

I engaged in homosexual activity or in unnatural sexual activities? Have I failed to protect the sexual innocence of children? Do I see the value of my own sexual integrity? Do I dress modestly?

You shall not steal. You shall not covet your neighbor's goods.

Have I taken possession of something that did not belong to me? Have I done damage to the property of another? Have I withheld money or property that is owed to another? Have I caused others to pay excessively for goods or services? Have I cheated another out of property, money, or rights? Have I gambled so as to risk being unable to provide for myself and my family? Have I squandered money in addictive spending? Have I cheated? Do I promote fair labor practices and just compensation? Do I honor my contracts? Am I responsible, working diligently for the pay I receive? Do I share with the poor according to my ability? Have I misused natural resources? Am I obsessed with envy for what another has? Am I greedy, desiring more than I need? Do I have a desire to amass wealth and goods without limit? Do I hoard? Do I feel so envious that I become sad or frustrated at another's happiness or success? Do I wish harm or failure to someone who is more successful than I? Do I wish misfortune to another so that I will somehow profit? Do I seek the power that may accompany wealth?

You shall not bear false witness against your neighbor.

Have I lied or willfully deceived another? Have I committed perjury by lying under oath? Have I hurt another's good name by revealing negative facts about that person without proper reason (the sin of detraction)? Have I slandered anyone? Have I committed libel? Have I gossiped? Have I judged a person on circumstantial evidence or hearsay? Have I failed to make reparation for harm caused by a lie I told or for damage I caused to another's reputation? Have I revealed secrets that have been told to me? Have I broken a professional standard of confidentiality in the workplace?

Act of Contrition

O my God, I am heartily sorry for having offended you, and I detest all my sins, because of your just punishments, but most of all because they offend you, my God, who are all-good and deserving of all my love. I firmly resolve, with the help of your grace, to sin no more and to avoid the near occasions of sin.

Contrition can also be expressed in your own words, such as:

Jesus, I ask your forgiveness for my sins. I am sorry for offending you. Please help me to avoid all sin in the future.

Thanksgiving After Confession

Dear Lord, I thank you for this wonderful sacrament, through which you have forgiven all my sins and faults. Beyond all doubt, you are a generous and gracious God whose mercy is limitless. Thank you for giving me this fresh start. Grant me the graces I need to walk the straight and narrow road. When temptations come, help me to resist them. But if I fall again, I know that you will always be there to lift me up, dust me off, and gently point me in the right direction. Thank you for loving me and letting me experience the peace that only you can give me.

ANOINTING OF THE SICK

While this is not necessarily the case, it can happen that when we are seriously ill or as we near the end of our lives, the attacks of the devil become more aggressive. The evil one realizes that his time to tempt us away from God is running out. Thus, Jesus and his Church provide us with a sacrament of strength: The Anointing of the Sick. In its fullness, this sacrament includes sacramental Reconciliation and the reception of the Eucharist. The anointing of the forehead and the hands, done in the name of Jesus, renews the power of the Lord in us, strengthens our faith and hope, and nourishes our love. It is yet another powerful means of victory over the powers of darkness and contains in itself many wonderful blessings of forgiveness and peace.

Sacramentals

The Church also provides us with sacramentals. These are sacred signs that prepare us to be more open to the action of the Holy Spirit both in the reception of the sacraments and in the working of grace in our daily lives. A sacramental is first and foremost a blessing, often accompanied by a sign (e.g., the sign of the cross and/or the sprinkling of holy water). The blessing of persons, meals, places (such as our homes), and objects are all sacramentals. It is only after a religious object has been blessed that we can refer to it as a "sacramental."

Examples of sacramental objects are crucifixes, rosaries, scapulars, relics, religious icons and pictures, medals, and statues. Holy water is also a sacramental, as are blessed candles, oil, salt, palms, and ashes. Having physical objects like these can help us involve our body and senses in our prayer. The Holy Spirit can make use of these objects to remind us of God's nearness, move us to greater devotion and love of God, inspire holy thoughts, and awaken in our hearts the desire to do good and avoid evil. That's why they are so important for our spiritual life and why the devil hates them.

If you haven't used sacramental objects before, now is a good time to start. Some of those most powerful are the crucifix, the rosary, holy water, the scapular, the Miraculous Medal of Our Lady, and the Saint Benedict medal. They are especially effective against Satan because of both the blessing they carry and the spiritual reality they represent. They are also important personal reminders of the abiding presence and protection of God.

When you buy a religious object, have it blessed by a priest so that it becomes a sacramental. It's important to always carry a blessed object on your person (crucifix, medal, scapular, rosary . . .). Having religious objects visible in your home—for example, a crucifix as you enter, a framed picture of the Sacred Heart in the family room, a statue of Our Lady in the bedroom or the kitchen—is not merely for decoration. It is a declaration that you and your house belong to the Lord. Keep holy water in your home and use it to bless yourself; if you are a parent, bless your children before they go to bed. Sacramentals are one more way to sanctify our lives and grow in grace.

Especially to be recommended is the Enthronement of the Sacred Heart, a way of consecrating your heart and your home to Jesus. In an apparition to Saint Margaret Mary, Jesus said, "I will bless every place in which an image of my Heart is exposed and honored." It's a very simple act that will bring countless blessings to the home. You can set a date with your pastor, or if he is unable to come, you can do it yourself. There's ample information online as to how to do the enthronement.

II

God's Word

Another important means of defense is to know our faith and inform our conscience. Saint Paul tells us to "draw our strength from the Lord and from his mighty power" so that we can "stand firm against the tactics of the devil"; to "put on the armor of God" and take up the "sword of the Spirit, which is the word of God" (see Eph 6:10–16). This means we need to be familiar with God's word, to read the Bible and study the catechism. In this way we are better equipped to recognize evil and name it so that we can resist it; an informed conscience weathers storms better than one that is stumbling in darkness. When Jesus is tempted in the desert, he does not fall into the trap of getting into a discussion with the devil (never a good idea), but he does cut him off by quoting Scripture to him. If we are well versed in the word of God, meditating it with humility and a docile heart, it will come to our aid when we need it.

God's word is "living and effective, sharper than any two-edged sword," says the author of the Letter to the Hebrews, "penetrating even between soul and spirit, joints and marrow, and able to discern reflections and thoughts of the heart" (Heb 4:12). The more we read and take to heart the teachings of God in Sacred Scripture, the more we are able to recognize the workings of our own heart and mind and all that motivates us. We become more discerning in our choices, more desirous of good, more able to recognize the ruses of the evil one. The word of God fortifies us when we are weak; comforts us in distress; nourishes faith, hope, and love in us; and brings joy and light to our lives.

Keep a Bible in your home in a place where you can see it and, if possible, at work as well. Read a little bit every day.

Scripture Verses in Times of Temptation

Matthew 4:1–11

Matthew 16:24–28

Matthew 18:6–9

Mark 14:32–38

Luke 22:31–34

John 17:12–19

Romans 6:2–14

Romans 7:21–25

1 Corinthians
10:12–13

Ephesians 6:10–18

1 Timothy 6:12–16

Hebrews 2:17–18;
4:14–16

James 1:2–8, 12–18

James 4:1–10

1 Peter 5:6–11

1 John 4:1–3

Scripture Verses on the Power of God

Exodus 14:10–31

Isaiah 40:28–31

Isaiah 41:8–14

Matthew 8:23–27

Mark 1:21–28

Mark 6:45–52

Luke 6:17–19

Luke 10:17–20

John 11:17–44

Romans 8:31–39

2 Corinthians
12:7–10

Philippians 4:6–7,
13

Revelation 12:1–10

Psalms for Protection and Deliverance

Psalm 7

Psalm 23

Psalm 27

Psalm 28

Psalm 31

Psalm 32

Psalm 34

Psalm 40

Psalm 54

Psalm 57

Psalm 62

Psalm 68

Psalm 86

Psalm 91

Psalm 94

Psalm 121

Psalm 141

Psalm 143

III

Basic Prayers

A major means of defense is prayer. Prayer is extremely important, because it is in prayer that we develop a deep and lasting relationship with the Lord. Evil spirits will try to prevent this in every way possible. They will suggest that now is not a good time to pray, that you are too tired or too stressed, too busy or not in the right frame of mind. Sometimes the temptations are ever so subtle. There is nothing the devil wants more than to keep us from praying.

But the saints tell us that prayer is the first and most important means for deliverance and protection from evil.

The Sign of the Cross

The Sign of the Cross represents the victory of Jesus over evil and death. Saint John Vianney says that a well-made sign of the cross "makes all hell tremble." We use this sign both to bless ourselves and to ward off evil by tracing the cross of Christ over our body and proclaiming our faith in the three divine Persons.

We should begin and end our day with the Sign of the Cross. Saint John Chrysostom writes: "Never leave your house without making the sign of the cross. It will be to you a staff, a weapon, an impregnable fortress. Neither man nor demon will dare to attack you, seeing you covered with such powerful armor. Let this sign teach you that you are a soldier, ready to combat against the demons, and ready to fight for the crown of justice. Are you ignorant of what the cross has done? It has vanquished death, destroyed sin, emptied hell, dethroned Satan, and restored the universe. Would you doubt its power?"[1]

In nomine Patris, et Filii, et Spiritus Sancti. Amen.

In the name of the Father, and of the Son, and of the Holy Spirit. Amen.

The Lord's Prayer

This prayer is given us by Jesus himself, who taught his disciples to pray for deliverance from evil and focus all their love and attention on the Father and his will for them.

Pater Noster, qui es in caelis, sanctificetur nomen tuum. Adveniat regnum tuum. Fiat voluntas tua, sicut in caelo et in terra. Panem nostrum quotidianum da nobis hodie, et dimitte nobis debita nostra sicut et nos dimittimus debitoribus nostris. Et ne nos inducas in tentationem, sed libera nos a malo. Amen.

Our Father, who art in heaven, hallowed be thy name; thy kingdom come; thy will be done on earth as it is in heaven. Give us this day our daily bread, and forgive us our trespasses, as we forgive those who trespass against us, and lead us not into temptation, but deliver us from evil. Amen.

Hail Mary

Pope Francis never tires of urging the faithful to turn to Mary: "Mary guards our faith, protects relationships, saves us in stormy weather, and preserves us from evil."[2] The devil hates the Blessed Virgin and is afraid of her; he does not enter where she is present. Every time we invoke her, we wrap ourselves in her protective mantle.

Ave Maria, gratia plena, Dominus tecum. Benedicta tu in mulieribus, et benedictus fructus ventris tui, Iesus. Sancta Maria, Mater Dei, ora pro nobis peccatoribus, nunc, et in hora mortis nostrae. Amen.

Hail Mary, full of grace, the Lord is with thee. Blessed are thou among women, and blessed is the fruit of thy womb, Jesus. Holy Mary, Mother of God, pray for us sinners, now and at the hour of our death. Amen.

Glory Be

By repeating this prayer of praise in honor of the Most Holy Trinity, we unite ourselves to him. And the one united to God, says Saint John of the Cross, is feared by the devil as if it were God himself. Let this be our first prayer upon waking in the morning and our last prayer before falling asleep at night.

Gloria Patri, et Filio, et Spiritui Sancto. Sicut erat in principio, et nunc, et semper, et in saecula saeculorum. Amen.

Glory be to the Father and to the Son and to the Holy Spirit. As it was in the beginning, is now, and ever shall be, world without end. Amen.

The Apostles' Creed

Credo in Deum Patrem omnipotentem,
Creatorem caeli et terrae.
Et in Iesum Christum, Filium eius unicum,
Dominum nostrum,
qui conceptus est de Spiritu Sancto,
natus ex Maria Virgine, passus sub
    Pontio Pilato,
crucifixus, mortuus, et sepultus,
descendit ad infernos, tertia die resurrexit

a mortuis,
ascendit ad caelos, sedet ad dexteram Dei
    Patris omnipotentis,
inde venturus est iudicare vivos et mortuos.
Credo in Spiritum Sanctum, sanctam
    Ecclesiam catholicam,
sanctorum communionem, remissionem
    peccatorum,
carnis resurrectionem, vitam aeternam. Amen.

I believe in God, the Father Almighty, creator of heaven and earth.

I believe in Jesus Christ, his only Son, our Lord. He was conceived by the power of the Holy Spirit and born of the Virgin Mary. He suffered under Pontius Pilate, was crucified, died, and was buried. He descended into hell. On the third day he rose again. He ascended into heaven, and is seated at the right hand of the Father. He will come again to judge the living and the dead.

I believe in the Holy Spirit, the holy catholic Church, the communion of saints, the forgiveness of sins, the resurrection of the body, and life everlasting. Amen.

IV

Prayers to Jesus, Our Lord and Redeemer

The Name of Jesus

There is no name in heaven or on earth more powerful than the name of Jesus. Demons tremble at the sacred name of Jesus; simply saying his name devoutly puts them to flight. Pray the name of Jesus trustingly, humbly; he will protect and deliver you from all evil: "God greatly exalted him and bestowed on him the name that is above every name, that at the name of Jesus every knee should bend, of those in heaven and on earth and under the earth, and every tongue confess that Jesus Christ is Lord, to the glory of God the Father" (Phil 2:9–11).

Litany of the Holy Name of Jesus

Lord, *have mercy.*

Christ, *have mercy.*

Lord, *have mercy.*

Jesus, *hear us.*

Jesus, *graciously hear us.*

Response: have mercy on us.

God the Father of heaven, *R.*

God the Son, Redeemer of the world, *R.*

God the Holy Spirit, *R.*

Holy Trinity, one God, *R.*

Jesus, Son of the living God, *R.*

Jesus, splendor of the Father, *R.*

Jesus, brightness of eternal light, *R.*

Jesus, king of glory, *R.*

Jesus, sun of justice, *R.*

Jesus, Son of the Virgin Mary, *R.*

Jesus, most amiable, *R.*

Jesus, most admirable, *R.*

Jesus, the mighty God, *R.*

Jesus, father of the world to come, *R.*

Jesus, wonderful counselor, *R.*

Jesus, most powerful, *R.*

Jesus, most patient, *R.*

Jesus, most obedient, *R.*

Jesus, meek and humble of heart, *R.*

Jesus, lover of chastity, *R.*

Jesus, lover of us all, *R.*

Jesus, God of peace, *R.*

Jesus, author of life, *R.*

Jesus, example of virtue, *R.*

Jesus, ardent lover of souls, *R.*

Jesus, our God, *R.*

Jesus, our refuge, *R.*

Jesus, father of the poor, *R.*

Jesus, treasure of the faithful, *R.*

Jesus, Good Shepherd, *R.*

Jesus, true light, *R.*

Jesus, eternal wisdom, *R.*

Jesus, infinite goodness, *R.*

Jesus, our way and our life, *R.*

Jesus, joy of the angels, *R.*

Jesus, king of the patriarchs, *R.*

Jesus, master of the apostles, *R.*

Jesus, teacher of the evangelists, *R.*

Jesus, strength of martyrs, *R.*

Jesus, light of confessors, *R.*

Jesus, purity of virgins, *R.*

Jesus, crown of all saints, *R.*

Be merciful, *spare us, O Jesus.*

Be merciful, *graciously hear us, O Jesus.*

   Response: *deliver us, O Jesus.*

From every evil, *R.*

From all sin, *R.*

From your anger, *R.*

From the snares of the devil, *R.*

From the spirit of impurity, *R.*

From everlasting death, *R.*

From neglect of your inspirations, *R.*

By the mystery of your incarnation, *R.*

By your birth, *R.*

By your infancy, *R.*

By your life and ministry, *R.*

By your agony and abandonment, *R.*

By your sufferings and crucifixion, *R.*

By your death and burial, *R.*

By your resurrection from the dead, *R.*

By your ascension into heaven, *R.*

By your gift of the Holy Eucharist, *R.*

By your joy and glory, *R.*

Lamb of God, who take away the sins of the world, *spare us, O Jesus.*

Lamb of God, who take away the sins of the world, *graciously hear us, O Jesus.*

Lamb of God, who take away the sins of the world, *have mercy on us, O Jesus.*

Jesus, *hear us.*

Jesus, *graciously hear us.*

Let us pray.

O Lord Jesus Christ, you have said, "Ask and you shall receive; seek, and you shall find; knock, and it shall be opened to you" (see Mt 7:7); mercifully grant us the grace of your divine love and a reverence for your holy name, that we may love you with all our hearts and in all our words and actions, and never cease to praise you, who live and reign forever and ever. Amen.

Anima Christi

Soul of Christ sanctify me.
Body of Christ save me.
Blood of Christ inebriate me.
Water from the side of Christ wash me.
Passion of Christ strengthen me.
O good Jesus hear me.
Within your wounds hide me.
Permit me not to be separated from you.
From the malignant enemy defend me.
In the hour of my death call me.
And bid me come to you,
that with your saints I may praise you
forever and ever. Amen.

Litany of the Most Precious Blood of Jesus

Lord, *have mercy.*

Christ, *have mercy.*

Lord, *have mercy.*

Christ, *hear us.*

Christ, *graciously hear us.*

Response: have mercy on us.

God, the Father of heaven,

God, the Son, Redeemer of the world, *R.*

God, the Holy Spirit, *R.*

Holy Trinity, One God, *R.*

Response: save us.

Blood of Christ, only-begotten Son of the
eternal Father, *R.*

Blood of Christ, Incarnate Word of God, *R.*

Blood of Christ, of the new and eternal
covenant, *R.*

Blood of Christ, spilled upon the earth in the
agony, *R.*

Blood of Christ, shed profusely in the
scourging, *R.*

Blood of Christ, flowing forth in the crowning
with thorns, *R.*

Blood of Christ, poured out on the cross, *R.*

Blood of Christ, price of our redemption, *R.*

Blood of Christ, offering forgiveness and
pardon for sin, *R.*

Blood of Christ, Eucharistic refreshment
   of souls, *R.*

Blood of Christ, river of mercy, *R.*

Blood of Christ, victor over evil, *R.*

Blood of Christ, courage of martyrs, *R.*

Blood of Christ, strength of confessors, *R.*

Blood of Christ, sustenance of virgins, *R.*

Blood of Christ, help of those in peril, *R.*

Blood of Christ, relief of the burdened, *R.*

Blood of Christ, solace in sorrow, *R.*

Blood of Christ, hope of the repentant, *R.*

Blood of Christ, consolation of the dying, *R.*

Blood of Christ, peace and comfort of hearts, *R.*

Blood of Christ, pledge of eternal life, *R.*

Blood of Christ, freeing souls from purgatory, *R.*

Blood of Christ, most worthy of all glory and
   honor, *R.*

Lamb of God, who take away the sins of the
   world, *spare us, O Lord.*

Lamb of God, who take away the sins of the
   world, *graciously hear us, O Lord.*

Lamb of God, who take away the sins of the world, *have mercy on us.*

V. You have redeemed us by your Blood, O Lord.

R. And made us a kingdom to serve our God.

Let us pray.

Almighty and eternal God, you gave your only-begotten Son to us to be our Redeemer. Grant that his saving Blood be a safeguard against every evil, so that we may rejoice in its fruits forever in heaven. Through the same Christ our Lord. Amen.

Cleanse Me, Jesus

Lord Jesus Christ, I place myself at the foot of your cross and ask you to cover me with your Precious Blood which pours forth from your Most Sacred Heart and your Most Holy Wounds. Cleanse me, my Jesus, in the living water that flows from your Heart. I ask you to surround me with your holy light.

Act of Consecration to the Sacred Heart of Jesus

O Sacred Heart of Jesus, to you I consecrate and offer up my person and my life, my actions, trials, and sufferings, that my entire being may only be employed in loving, honoring, and glorifying you. This is my irrevocable will, to belong entirely to you, and to do all for your love, renouncing with my whole heart all that can displease you.

I take you, O Sacred Heart, for the sole object of my love, the protection of my life, the pledge of my salvation, the remedy of my frailty and inconstancy, the reparation for all the defects of my life, and my secure refuge at the hour of my death. O Most Merciful Heart, be my justification before God your Father, and screen me from his anger which I have so justly merited. I fear all from my own weakness and malice, but placing my entire confidence in you, O Heart of Love, I hope all from your infinite Goodness. Annihilate in me all that can displease or resist you. Imprint your pure love so deeply in my heart that I may never forget you or be separated from you.

I beseech you, through your infinite Goodness, grant that my name be engraved upon your Heart, for in this I place all my happiness and all my glory, to live and to die as one of your devoted servants. Amen.

Saint Margaret Mary Alacoque

Invocation to the Sacred Heart of Jesus

Lord Jesus, let my heart never rest until it finds you, who are its center, its love, and its happiness. By the wound in your Heart pardon the sins that I have committed whether out of malice or out of evil desires. Place my weak heart in your own divine Heart, continually under your protection and guidance, so that I may persevere in doing good and in fleeing evil until my last breath. Amen.

Saint Margaret Mary Alacoque

Litany of the Sacred Heart of Jesus

Lord, *have mercy on us.*

Christ, *have mercy on us.*

Lord, *have mercy on us.*

Response: *have mercy on us.*

God our Father in heaven, *R.*

God the Son, Redeemer of the world, *R.*

God the Holy Spirit, *R.*

Holy Trinity, one God, *R.*

Heart of Jesus, Son of the eternal Father, *R.*

Heart of Jesus, formed by the Holy Spirit in the womb of the Virgin Mother, *R.*

Heart of Jesus, one with the eternal Word, *R.*

Heart of Jesus, infinite in majesty, *R.*

Heart of Jesus, holy temple of God, *R.*

Heart of Jesus, tabernacle of the Most High, *R.*

Heart of Jesus, house of God and gate of heaven, *R.*

Heart of Jesus, aflame with love for us, *R.*

Heart of Jesus, source of justice and love, *R.*

Heart of Jesus, full of goodness and love, *R.*

Heart of Jesus, wellspring of all virtue, *R.*

Heart of Jesus, worthy of all praise, *R.*

Heart of Jesus, king and center of all hearts, *R.*

Heart of Jesus, treasure-house of wisdom and knowledge, *R.*

Heart of Jesus, in whom the fullness of divinity dwells, *R.*

Heart of Jesus, in whom the Father is well pleased, *R.*

Heart of Jesus, from whose fullness we have all received, *R.*

Heart of Jesus, desire of the everlasting hills, *R.*

Heart of Jesus, patient and full of mercy, *R.*

Heart of Jesus, generous to all who turn to you, *R.*

Heart of Jesus, fountain of life and holiness, *R.*

Heart of Jesus, atonement for our sins, *R.*

Heart of Jesus, weighed down with insults, *R.*

Heart of Jesus, bruised for our offenses, *R.*

Heart of Jesus, obedient even unto death, *R.*

Heart of Jesus, pierced by a lance, *R.*

Heart of Jesus, source of all consolation, *R.*

Heart of Jesus, our life and resurrection, *R.*

Heart of Jesus, our peace and reconciliation, *R.*

Heart of Jesus, victim for our sins, *R.*

Heart of Jesus, salvation of all who trust in you, *R.*

Heart of Jesus, hope of all who die in you, *R.*

Heart of Jesus, delight of all the saints, *R.*

Lamb of God, you take away the sins of the world, *spare us, O Lord.*

Lamb of God, you take away the sins of the world, *graciously hear us, O Lord.*

Lamb of God, you take away the sins of the world, *have mercy on us.*

V. Jesus, gentle and humble of heart.

R. Form our hearts and make them like your own.

Let us pray.

Father in heaven, we praise and thank you for the gifts of love we have received from the Heart of your Son, Jesus. Teach us to see Christ in those whose lives we touch and show our grateful love through service to our brothers and sisters. We ask this in the name of Jesus the Lord. Amen.

O Heart of Jesus

O Heart of Jesus, adored in heaven, invoked on earth, feared in hell: Reign over all hearts, reign throughout the ages, reign forever in heavenly glory. Amen.

Saint Gertrude the Great

To Our Lord Jesus

O Jesus, my Savior, my Lord and my God, my God and my all, with your sacrifice on the cross you redeemed us and defeated the power of Satan. I beg you to deliver me from every evil presence and every evil influence. I ask in your name, I ask you for the sake of your wounds, I ask you for the sake of your blood, I ask you for the sake of your cross, I ask you through the intercession of Mary, immaculate and sorrowful. May the blood and the water that flow from your side wash over me to purify me, deliver me, heal me. Amen.[3]

The Chaplet of Divine Mercy

(This may be prayed using a five-decade rosary.)

> Even if there were a sinner most hardened, if he
> were to recite this chaplet only once, he would
> receive grace from My infinite mercy.

Jesus to Saint Faustina Kowalska, Diary, 687

*Jesus himself dictated the Chaplet of Divine Mercy to
Saint Faustina Kowalska. In this prayer we offer Jesus—
Body, Blood, Soul, and Divinity—to God the Father,
and we unite ourselves with his sacrifice offered on the
cross for the salvation of the world. We ask for mercy for
ourselves and for all people: those living on earth and the
souls in purgatory.*

Begin with an Our Father, Hail Mary, and
Apostles' Creed.

On the single bead before each decade:

Eternal Father, I offer you the Body and
Blood, Soul and Divinity of your dearly beloved
Son, our Lord Jesus Christ, in atonement for our
sins and those of the whole world.

On the ten beads of each decade:

For the sake of his sorrowful passion, have mercy on us and on the whole world.

After the five decades, conclude with:

Holy God, Holy Mighty One, Holy Immortal One, have mercy on us and on the whole world (three times).

V

Prayers to God
the Holy Spirit

Prayer to the Holy Spirit

Holy Spirit, Lord and Giver of life, you who came down upon the apostles in a mighty wind and with fire, who filled the house where they were and gave them the gift of tongues to proclaim the wonders of God, come down now upon me also.

Fill me with yourself, and make of me a temple wherein you dwell. Open my lips to proclaim your praise, to ask your guidance, and to declare your love.

Holy Light, divine Fire, eternal Might, enlighten my mind to know you, inflame my heart to love you, strengthen my will to seek and find you.

Be for me the living and life-giving Breath of God, the very air I breathe, and the only sky in which my spirit soars.

Prayer for the Fruits of the Holy Spirit

Lord Jesus, by myself I can do nothing, but with the help of your grace I can do all things. And so, with all my heart:

— In the name of Jesus Christ, I reject the spirit of anger, and humbly implore the Holy Spirit for the virtues of meekness and gentleness.

— In the name of Jesus Christ, I reject the spirit of greed and implore the Holy Spirit for the virtue of generosity.

— In the name of Jesus Christ, I reject the spirit of sloth and implore the Holy Spirit for the virtues of diligence and fidelity.

— In the name of Jesus Christ, I reject the spirit of pride and implore the Holy Spirit for the virtues of humility and poverty of spirit.

— In the name of Jesus Christ, I reject the spirit of lust and implore the Holy Spirit for the virtues of chastity and purity of heart.

— In the name of Jesus Christ, I reject the spirit of gluttony and implore the Holy Spirit for the virtues of temperance and self-control.

— In the name of Jesus Christ, I reject the spirit of envy and implore the Holy Spirit for the virtues of charity, joy, and peace.

Heal Me, Holy Spirit

Holy Spirit, through the intercession of the Queen of Pentecost:

Heal my mind of lack of reflection, ignorance, forgetfulness, obstinacy, prejudice, error, and perversion, and form Jesus Christ-Truth in everything.

Heal my heart of indifference, diffidence, bad inclinations, passions, overly sentimental feelings, and attachments, and form Jesus Christ-Life in everything.

Heal my will of lack of willpower, fickleness, inconstancy, sloth, stubbornness, and bad habits, and form Jesus Christ-Way in me.

Give me a new love for whatever Jesus loves and for Jesus himself.

Let there be a new Pentecost and let me be a new apostle, gifted with the spirit of wisdom, knowledge, understanding, counsel, piety, fortitude, and holy fear of God.

Blessed James Alberione

VI

Prayers to the
Most Blessed Virgin Mary

The Holy Rosary

*After the Holy Sacrifice of the Mass, the most power-
ful prayer of protection and deliverance is the Rosary.
Fr. Gabriele Amorth, SSP, chief exorcist for the Vatican,
is known to have said, "Anyone who goes to Mary and
prays the Rosary cannot be touched by Satan."*

*In fact, Fr. Amorth tells the story that one day a
colleague of his heard the devil say during an exorcism:
"Every Hail Mary is like a blow to my head. If Christians knew how powerful the Rosary is, it would be my
end."[4]*

> At least a fourth part of the Rosary is to be said
> every day; better, two parts; best of all, the entire
> Rosary. Keep a blessed rosary with you, day and
> night. Reflect on the mysteries as you pray.
>
> *Blessed James Alberione*

Begin the Rosary by making the Sign of the
Cross (p. 41); then, while holding the crucifix,
pray the Apostles' Creed (p. 44). On the beads

following the crucifix pray one Our Father (p. 41), three Hail Marys (p. 42), and a Glory Be to the Father (p. 43). Next, read the mystery and pray one Our Father, ten Hail Marys, and a Glory Be to the Father. It is recommended to then pray the Fatima Prayer (p. 77). This completes one decade. All the other decades are prayed in the same manner, while pondering the mystery for each decade. Pray the Hail Holy Queen (p. 77) at the end and, if you wish, the Litany of Loreto (p. 77).

1. Make the Sign of the Cross and pray the Apostles' Creed.
2. Pray the Our Father.
3. Pray 3 Hail Marys.
4. Pray the Glory, name the first Mystery, and pray the Our Father.
5. Pray 10 Hail Marys.
6. Pray the Glory, name the second Mystery, and pray the Our Father.
7. Repeat steps 5 and 6 with each Mystery until you reach the end.
8. Pray the Glory and the Hail, Holy Queen.

JOYFUL MYSTERIES

1. The Annunciation of the Angel to Mary
   (Lk 1:26–38)

2. Mary Visits Her Cousin Elizabeth
   (Lk 1:39–40)

3. The Birth of Jesus at Bethlehem
   (Lk 2:1–14)

4. The Presentation of Jesus in the Temple
   (Lk 2:22–34)

5. The Finding of Jesus in the Temple
   (Lk 2:42–48)

LUMINOUS MYSTERIES

1. John Baptizes Jesus in the Jordan
   (Mt 3:13–17)

2. Christ Reveals His Glory at the
   Wedding at Cana (Jn 2:1–11)

3. Jesus Proclaims the Kingdom of God and
   Calls Us to Conversion
   (Mk 1:14–15)

4. The Transfiguration of Jesus
   (Mk 9:2–8)

5. Jesus Institutes the Eucharist
   (Mk 14:22–25)

Sorrowful Mysteries

1. Jesus Prays in the Garden of Gethsemane
   (Mk 14:32–42)
2. Jesus Is Scourged
   (Mk 15:15)
3. Jesus Is Crowned with Thorns
   (Mt 27:27–31)
4. Jesus Carries the Cross to Calvary
   (Lk 23:26–32)
5. Jesus Is Crucified
   (Lk 23:33–49; Jn 19:25–27)

Glorious Mysteries

1. Jesus Rises from the Dead
   (Mt 28:1–6)
2. Jesus Ascends into Heaven
   (Acts 1:9–11)
3. The Holy Spirit Descends on Mary and the
   Apostles (Acts 2:1–4)
4. Mary Is Assumed into Heaven
   (Jn 14:3)
5. Mary Is Crowned Queen of Heaven and
   Earth (Rev 12:1)

Fatima Prayer

O my Jesus, forgive us our sins. Save us from the fires of hell. Lead all souls to heaven, especially those who have most need of your mercy.

Hail Holy Queen

Hail, holy Queen, Mother of mercy, our life, our sweetness, and our hope! To you do we cry, poor banished children of Eve. To you do we send up our sighs, mourning, and weeping in this valley of tears. Turn, then, most gracious advocate, your eyes of mercy toward us; and after this our exile, show unto us the blessed fruit of your womb, Jesus. O clement, O loving, O sweet Virgin Mary.

Litany of Loreto

Lord, *have mercy on us.*
Christ, *have mercy on us.*
Lord, *have mercy on us.*
Christ, *hear us.*
Christ, *graciously hear us.*

Response: have mercy on us.

God, the Father of heaven, *R.*

God the Son, Redeemer of the world, *R.*

God the Holy Spirit, *R.*

Holy Trinity, one God, *R.*

Response: pray for us.

Holy Mary, *R.*

Holy Mother of God, *R.*

Holy Virgin of virgins, *R.*

Mother of Christ, *R.*

Mother of the Church, *R.*

Mother of mercy, *R.*

Mother of divine grace, *R.*

Mother of hope, *R.*

Mother most pure, *R.*

Mother most chaste, *R.*

Mother inviolate, *R.*

Mother undefiled, *R.*

Mother most amiable, *R.*

Mother most admirable, *R.*

Mother of good counsel, *R.*

Mother of our Creator, *R.*

Mother of our Redeemer, *R.*

Virgin most prudent, *R.*

Virgin most venerable, *R.*

Virgin most renowned, *R.*

Virgin most powerful, *R.*

Virgin most merciful, *R.*

Virgin most faithful, *R.*

Mirror of justice, *R.*

Seat of wisdom, *R.*

Cause of our joy, *R.*

Spiritual vessel, *R.*

Vessel of honor, *R.*

Singular vessel of devotion, *R.*

Mystical rose, *R.*

Tower of David, *R.*

Tower of ivory, *R.*

House of gold, *R.*

Ark of the Covenant, *R.*

Gate of heaven, *R.*

Morning star, *R.*

Health of the sick, *R.*

Refuge of sinners, *R.*

Solace of migrants, *R.*

Comforter of the afflicted, *R.*

Help of Christians, *R.*

Queen of Angels, *R.*

Queen of Patriarchs, *R.*

Queen of Prophets, *R.*

Queen of Apostles, *R.*

Queen of Martyrs, *R.*

Queen of Confessors, *R.*

Queen of Virgins, *R.*

Queen of all Saints, *R.*

Queen conceived without original sin, *R.*

Queen assumed into heaven, *R.*

Queen of the most holy Rosary, *R.*

Queen of families, *R.*

Queen of peace, *R.*

Lamb of God, who takes away the sins of the
world, *spare us, O Lord.*

Lamb of God, who takes away the sins of the
world, *graciously hear us, O Lord.*

Lamb of God, who takes away the sins of the world, *have mercy on us.*

   V. Pray for us, O holy Mother of God.
   R. That we may be made worthy of the promises of Christ.

Let us pray.

Grant your servants continual health of mind and body, O Lord God. Let the intercession of the Blessed ever-Virgin Mary gain for us freedom from our present sorrow. Give us the joy of ever-lasting happiness. We ask this through Christ our Lord. Amen.

We Fly to Your Protection

We fly to your protection, O holy Mother of God.

Despise not our petitions in our necessities, but deliver us always from all dangers, O glorious and blessed Virgin.

> *Oldest known prayer to the Virgin,*
> *found on a Greek papyrus, ca. 300*

The Memorare

Remember, O most gracious Virgin Mary, that never was it known that anyone who fled to your protection, implored your help, or sought your intercession was left unaided. Inspired by this confidence, I fly unto you, O Virgin of virgins, my mother; to you do I come, before you I stand, sinful and sorrowful. O Mother of the Word Incarnate, despise not my petitions, but in your mercy hear and answer me. Amen.

Attributed to Saint Bernard of Clairvaux

Prayer to Our Mother of Mercy

Virgin full of goodness, Mother of mercy, I entrust to you my body and my soul, my thoughts and my actions, my life and my death. O my Queen, come to my aid and deliver me from the snares of evil. Obtain for me the grace to love my Lord Jesus Christ, your Son, with a true and perfect love, and after him, O Mary, to love you with all my heart and above all things. Amen.

Saint Thomas Aquinas

Prayer to the Holy Virgin, Mother of Sorrows

Most Holy Mother of Sorrows, by the suffering you endured at the foot of the cross during the hours of your Son's agony, assist us in our final hours. Intercede for us so that after we pass from this life we may be admitted to the joys of paradise.

(Pray three Hail Marys.)

Mother of mercy, mother of grace,
Mary, help a fallen race;
Shield us when the foe is nigh,
And receive us when we die.

V. From sudden and unprepared death,
R. Deliver us, O Lord.
V. From the snares of the devil,
R. Deliver us, O Lord.
V. From everlasting death,
R. Deliver us, O Lord.

Let us pray.

O God, for the salvation of the human race, you gave us, in the passion and death of your

Son, an example and a refuge. Grant us, we pray, that at the final hour of our death we may be made partakers of our Redeemer's glory. Through the same Christ our Lord. Amen.

Rosary of the Seven Sorrows of Mary

The Rosary of the Seven Sorrows of Mary is an ancient devotion that focuses on Mary's maternal love and her participation in the sufferings and death of Jesus. Having experienced such great suffering in her own life, Mary is full of compassion for us in our own trials.

Begin by praying an act of contrition, then announce the first sorrow, and pray one Our Father and seven Hail Marys while meditating on the mystery. Continue for all seven sorrows and conclude by praying three additional Hail Marys, in honor of our Lady's tears, and the closing prayer.

First Sorrow: The Prophecy of Simeon

Simeon blessed them and said to his mother, Mary, "Behold, he is destined to bring about the fall and rise of many in Israel, and to be a sign that will be opposed. And a sword shall pierce your own soul, so that the thoughts of many hearts may be revealed" (Lk 2:34–35).

I grieve for you, O Mary most sorrowful, in the affliction of your tender heart at the prophecy of the holy and aged Simeon. Dear Mother, by your heart so afflicted, obtain for me the virtue of humility and the gift of holy fear of the Lord.

Second Sorrow: The Flight into Egypt

When they had departed, behold, the angel of the Lord appeared in a dream to Joseph and said, "Get up, take the child and its mother and flee to Egypt and stay there until I tell you—Herod is going to search for the child to kill it." So [Joseph] got up and took the child and his mother and departed by night for Egypt, and he stayed there until Herod's death . . . (Mt 2:13–15).

I grieve for you, O Mary most sorrowful, in the anguish of your most loving heart during the flight into Egypt and your sojourn there. Dear Mother, by your heart so troubled, obtain for me the virtue of generosity, especially toward the poor, and the gift of piety.

Third Sorrow: The Loss of Jesus
in Jerusalem

His mother said to him, "Son, why did you do this to us? You see your father and I have been looking for you and worrying!" (Lk 2:48).

I grieve for you, O Mary most sorrowful, in the anxieties that tried your troubled heart at the loss of your dear Jesus. Dear Mother, by your heart so full of anguish, obtain for me the virtue of chastity and the gift of knowledge.

Fourth Sorrow: Mary Meets Jesus
on the Way of the Cross

Is it nothing to you, all you who pass by? Look and see if there is any sorrow like my sorrow (Lam 1:12).

I grieve for you, O Mary most sorrowful, in the pain of your heart when you met Jesus as he carried his cross. Dear Mother, by your heart so troubled, obtain for me the virtue of patience and the gift of fortitude.

Fifth Sorrow: Mary Stands at the Foot of the Cross

Now standing by Jesus' cross were his mother and his mother's sister, Mary the wife of Clopas, and Mary Magdalen. When Jesus saw his mother and the disciple he loved standing by he said to his mother, "Woman, here is your son." Then he said to the disciple, "Here is your mother" (Jn 19:25–27).

I grieve for you, O Mary most sorrowful, in the martyrdom your generous heart endured when you stood near Jesus in his agony. Dear Mother, by your afflicted heart, obtain for me the virtue of temperance and the gift of counsel.

Sixth Sorrow: The Body of Jesus Is Taken Down from the Cross

One of the soldiers stabbed him in the side with a spear, and at once blood and water came out (Jn 19:34).

I grieve for you, O Mary most sorrowful, in the wounding of your compassionate heart when the side of Jesus was pierced by the lance before his body was removed from the cross. Dear Mother, by your heart thus transfixed, obtain for me the virtue of neighborly charity and the gift of understanding.

Seventh Sorrow: The Body of Jesus Is Placed in the Tomb

Joseph of Arimathea came to Pilate and asked for Jesus' body, and after taking it down he wrapped it in a linen shroud and placed it in a tomb hewn out of rock (Lk 23:52–53).

I grieve for you, O Mary most sorrowful, for the pangs that wrenched your most loving heart at the burial of Jesus. Dear Mother, by your heart sunk in the bitterness of desolation, obtain for me the virtue of diligence and the gift of wisdom.

Closing Prayer

V. Pray for us, O most sorrowful Virgin.
R. That we may be made worthy of the promises of Christ.

Let us pray. Lord Jesus, at the foot of the cross, the heart of your most holy Mother, the

Blessed Virgin Mary, was pierced with sorrow. May your Mother intercede for us before the throne of your mercy for our present needs, and at the hour of our death. Amen.

VII

Prayers to Saint Joseph, Guardian of the Holy Family and Terror of Demons

To You, O Blessed Joseph

To you, O blessed Joseph, we have recourse in our affliction, and having implored the help of your thrice holy spouse, we now, with hearts filled with confidence, earnestly beg you also to take us under your protection.

Defend, O most watchful guardian of the Holy Family, the chosen offspring of Jesus Christ. Keep from us, O most loving Father, all blight of error and corruption. Aid us from on high, most valiant defender, in this conflict with the powers of darkness. And even as of old you rescued the Child Jesus from the peril of his life, so now defend God's Holy Church from the snares of the enemy and from all adversity. Shield us ever under your patronage, that, following your example and strengthened by your help, we may live a holy life, die a happy death, and attain to everlasting bliss in heaven. Amen.

Pope Leo XIII

In Time of Need

Saint Joseph, patron of all who serve God in simplicity of heart and steadfast devotion, ask the Lord to fill my heart with the fire of his love. Awaken within me the virtues of integrity, reverence, and kindness, so that I may radiate God's love to everyone around me. Intercede for me in my time of particular need and obtain for me the favor I ask *(mention your request)*. Blessed Joseph, defend me against the forces of evil that lay in wait at every turn, be my protector in life and my consoler at the moment of death. Amen.

For Defense Against the Powers of Evil

Saint Joseph, defender against the powers of evil, with your mighty staff protect us against the devil and his minions. With Jesus and Mary, you fled through the night to avoid the wicked designs of Herod; now through the power of God, strike out against the evil spirits that try to ensnare the followers of Jesus Christ. Grant special protection, we pray, for children, parents, families, for priests and religious and the dying. By God's grace, no demon dares approach while you are near, so we implore you, always be near to us! Amen.

VIII

Prayers to the Angels
for Protection

To My Guardian Angel

Angel of God, my guardian dear, to whom God's love entrusts me here, ever this day/night be at my side, to light and guard, to rule and guide. Amen.

Daily Invocations to the Guardian Angel

Holy Angel, my protector:
From every sin, *guard and preserve me.*
From every danger, *guard and preserve me.*
From every snare of the devil, *guard and preserve me.*
From enemies visible and invisible, *guard and preserve me.*
From the works of darkness, *guard and preserve me.*
From hardness of heart, *guard and preserve me.*
From sudden death, *guard and preserve me.*
From eternal death, *guard and preserve me.*

Prayer to Saint Michael

Saint Michael the Archangel, defend us in battle; be our defense against the wickedness and snares of the devil. May God rebuke him, we humbly pray. And do thou, O prince of the heavenly host, by the power of God thrust into hell Satan and all the evil spirits who prowl about the world seeking the ruin of souls. Amen.

Litany of Saint Michael

Lord, *have mercy.*

Christ, *have mercy.*

Lord, *have mercy.*

Christ, *hear us.*

Christ, *graciously hear us.*

> *Response: have mercy on us.*

God, the Father of heaven, *R.*

God, the Son, Redeemer of the world, *R.*

God, the Holy Spirit, *R.*

Holy Trinity, one God, *R.*

> *Response: pray for us.*

Holy Mary, Queen of Angels, *R.*

Saint Michael, *R.*

Saint Michael, abundant font of divine wisdom, *R.*

Saint Michael, most perfect adorer of the Divine Word, *R.*

Saint Michael, whom God crowned with honor and glory, *R.*

Saint Michael, most powerful prince of the heavenly host, *R.*

Saint Michael, standard-bearer of the Most Holy Trinity, *R.*

Saint Michael, guardian of paradise, *R.*

Saint Michael, guide and consoler of the People of God, *R.*

Saint Michael, splendor and fortitude of the Church Militant, *R.*

Saint Michael, honor and joy of the Church Triumphant, *R.*

Saint Michael, light of the angels, *R.*

Saint Michael, protection of orthodox people, *R.*

Saint Michael, strength of those who fight under the standard of the cross, *R.*

Saint Michael, light and hope of souls near death, *R.*

Saint Michael, our most sure aid, *R.*

Saint Michael, help in our adversities, *R.*

Saint Michael, herald of the everlasting judgment, *R.*

Saint Michael, consoler of souls languishing in purgatory, *R.*

Saint Michael, receiver of the souls of the elect after death, *R.*

Saint Michael, our prince, *R.*

Saint Michael, our defender, *R.*

Lamb of God, who take away the sins of the word, *spare us, O Lord.*

Lamb of God, who take away the sins of the word, *graciously hear us, O Lord.*

Lamb of God, who take away the sins of the word, *have mercy on us.*

V. Pray for us, Saint Michael the Archangel.
R. That we may be made worthy of the promises of Christ.

Let us pray.

O Lord Jesus Christ, may your continual blessing sanctify us, and grant us, through the intercession of Saint Michael, the wisdom that teaches us to lay up our treasure in heaven and choose eternal goods over those of this world. You who lives and reigns forever. Amen.

Chaplet of Saint Michael the Archangel

When we pray the Chaplet of Saint Michael, we invoke the assistance of Saint Michael and the nine choirs of angels for protection against the forces of evil.

The chaplet is composed of nine sets of three beads, with one bead in between each set. On the single beads, pray an invocation and one Our Father; on each of the three beads, pray the Hail Mary.

Begin the Chaplet with the Sign of the Cross and the words:

V. O God come to my assistance.

R. O Lord make haste to help me.

Glory Be . . .

First Invocation

Through the intercession of Saint Michael and the Celestial choir of Seraphim, may the Lord make us worthy to burn with the fire of perfect charity.

1 Our Father, 3 Hail Marys

Second Invocation

Through the intercession of Saint Michael and the Celestial choir of Cherubim, may the Lord grant us grace to leave the ways of wickedness and run in the paths of Christian perfection.

1 Our Father, 3 Hail Marys

Third Invocation

Through the intercession of Saint Michael and the Celestial choir of Thrones, may the Lord infuse into our hearts a true and sincere spirit of humility.

1 Our Father, 3 Hail Marys

Fourth Invocation

Through the intercession of Saint Michael and the Celestial choir of Dominions, may the Lord give us grace to govern our senses and subdue our unruly passions.

1 Our Father, 3 Hail Marys

Fifth Invocation

Through the intercession of Saint Michael and the Celestial choir of Powers, may the Lord protect us, body and soul, against the snares and temptations of the devil.

1 Our Father, 3 Hail Marys

Sixth Invocation

Through the intercession of Saint Michael and the Celestial choir of Virtues, may God preserve us from evil and be our safeguard against temptation.

1 Our Father, 3 Hail Marys

SEVENTH INVOCATION

Through the intercession of Saint Michael and the Celestial choir of Principalities, may the Lord fill our souls with a true spirit of obedience.

1 Our Father, 3 Hail Marys

EIGHTH INVOCATION

Through the intercession of Saint Michael and the Celestial choir of Archangels, may God grant us perseverance in faith and good works in order that we gain the glory of Paradise.

1 Our Father, 3 Hail Marys

NINTH INVOCATION

Through the intercession of Saint Michael and the Celestial choir of Angels, may the Lord grant us their protection in this mortal life and to be conducted by them hereafter to eternal glory.

1 Our Father, 3 Hail Marys

In conclusion, pray four Our Fathers to honor Saint Michael, Saint Gabriel, Saint Raphael, and your guardian angel.

The Chaplet is concluded with the following prayers:

O glorious Prince Saint Michael,
chief and commander of the heavenly hosts,
guardian of souls,
vanquisher of rebel spirits,
servant in the house of the Divine King,
and our admirable conductor,
thou who dost shine with excellence and
superhuman virtue,
vouchsafe to deliver us from all evil,
who turn to thee with confidence,
and enable us by thy gracious protection
to serve God more and more faithfully every
day. Amen.

V. Pray for us, O Glorious Saint Michael,
    Prince of the Church of Jesus Christ.

R. That we may be made worthy of his
    promises.

PRAYER

Almighty and everlasting God,
who by a prodigy of Goodness
and a merciful desire
for the salvation of all men,
has appointed the most glorious Archangel
    Saint Michael,
Prince of your Church,
make us worthy,
we beseech you,
to be delivered by his powerful protection
from all our enemies,
that none of them may harass us
at the hour of our death,
but that we may be conducted by him
into the august presence of your Divine
    Majesty.
This we beg through the merits of Jesus
Christ our Lord. Amen.

IX

Prayers to the Saints
for Help and Protection

The Saint Benedict Medal

The Saint Benedict medal that is in use today was cast for the fourteen hundredth anniversary of the saint's birth. Many miracles have been attributed to this medal. The prayers engraved on it offer special protection from evil and the medal itself depicts miraculous moments from the life of Saint Benedict.

On the front side is Saint Benedict. In his right hand he is holding a cross, symbolic of the victory over sin and death won for us by Christ's passion and death. In his left hand is a book representing the *Rule of Saint Benedict*.

Beneath the cross is a chalice with a snake slithering out of it, referring to the attempt made on his life by one of the monks who tried to poison him. When Benedict blessed the cup with the sign of the cross, the cup broke and the wine spilled, saving Benedict's life. On the opposite side, under the book is a raven with a piece of bread in its claw. This is in reference to another murder attempt, when someone poisoned the bread that was served to the saint. Before he could eat it, a bird flew in the window and took it away.

Around this image are the words:

Crux Sancti Patris Benedicti (The cross of our Holy Father Benedict) and

Eius in obitu nostro praesentia nuniamur (May we be strengthened by his presence in the hour of our death).

On the reverse side we find the word PAX (peace) at the very top and a number of letters following the outside rim of the medal (from right to left):

VRS —*Vade Retro Satana* (Be gone, Satan)

NSMV —*Numquam Suade Mihi Vana* (Never tempt me with your vanities)

SMQL —*Sunt Mala Quae Libas* (What you offer me is evil)

IVB —*Ipse Venena Bibas* (Drink the poison yourself)

The interior of the medal has more letters. In the four circles are:

CSPB — *Crux Sancti Patris Benedicti* (The cross of our Holy Father Benedict);

vertically:

CSSML — *Crux Sacra Sit Mihi Lux* (May the holy cross be my light);

and horizontally:

NDSMD — *Numquam Draco Sit Mihi Dux* (May the dragon never be my guide).

Prayer to Saint Benedict

Dear Saint Benedict, I thank God for showering you with his grace to love him above all else and to establish a monastic rule that has helped so many of his children live full and holy lives.

Through the cross of Jesus Christ, I ask you to please intercede that God might protect me, my loved ones, my home, property, possessions, and workplace today and always by your holy blessing, that we may never be separated from Jesus,

Mary, and the company of all the blessed. Through your intercession may we be delivered from temptation, spiritual oppression, physical ills, and disease. Protect us from drug and alcohol abuse, impurity and immorality, objectionable companions, and negative attitudes. I ask this in Jesus' name. Amen.

To Saint Mary Magdalene

The Gospels tell us that Jesus freed Mary Magdalene of seven demons (see Mk 16:9; Lk 8:2). Mary of Magdala recognized her need and opened herself to the healing powers of Jesus Christ with faith and trust. From that moment on, she lived the teachings of Jesus so completely as to become a formidable enemy of Satan.

Merciful Father, your blessed Son restored Mary Magdalene to health of mind and body, delivering her from the demons that plagued her. Grant that through her intercession and by your grace we may be healed of all our infirmities and unhealthy attachments, protected from all evil and every assault of Satan. We ask this through Jesus Christ, your Son, our Lord, who lives and reigns with you and the Holy Spirit, one God, now and forever. Amen.

To Saint Anthony, Abbot

Saint Anthony of Egypt, Abbot, is renowned for his victory over the demons that attacked him in his desert cell. His weapons were prayer and penance.

Saint Anthony, Abbot, ancient and noble saint, we honor you as our intercessor and model of Christian love and total abandonment to God. In your love and dedication to the Lord, you left everything and followed our Lord into the desert.

The Church honors you greatly for your devout and austere way of life, a life dedicated to God and humanity. By your devotion to the Master, you vanquished the evil one and with your eloquence, you refuted heretics.

Because of your close friendship with God, the early Church invoked your intercession with great benefit for the salvation of souls and against the onslaught of all kinds of evil and diseases.

Grant us, who strive to follow the same Lord and Master, your special intercession and help against the onslaught of the evil one and against all temptations of the flesh, sicknesses, epidemics and pandemics, and every kind of division and heresy, both within and against the Church of God. May we be able to lead a life of close union with Jesus our Lord. Pray that we may be a true witness to the grace of Baptism, renewed at every Eucharistic encounter, and respond to his constant call and invitation by leading a life of self-discipline and generous sacrifice, a life dedicated and devoted to God and his holy will. Amen.

To Saint Teresa of Avila

In chapter 31 of her autobiography, Saint Teresa recounts this episode: "I was once in an oratory; and [the devil] appeared to me in an abominable form at my left side. . . . It seemed that a great flame, all bright without shadow, came forth from his body. He told me in a terrifying way that I had really freed myself from his hands, but he would catch me with them again."[5] Teresa goes

on to say that the devil disappeared, but immediately re-
turned again—twice! She didn't know what to do, so she
threw holy water at him and he disappeared for good.
"From long experience," she says, "I have learned that
there is nothing like holy water to put devils to flight
and prevent them from coming back again."[6]

O Saint Teresa, seraphic virgin, beloved spouse of your crucified Lord, on earth you burned with a love so intense toward God, and now you glow with a brighter and purer flame in paradise: obtain for me too, I beseech you, a spark of that same holy fire which shall cause me to forget the world, all things created, and even myself; for you always avidly desired to see Jesus loved by everyone. Grant that my every thought, desire, and affection may be continually directed to doing the will of God, the supreme Good, whether I am in joy or in pain, for he is worthy to be loved and obeyed forever. Obtain for me this grace, you who are so powerful with God; may I, like you, be all on fire with the holy love of God. Amen.

Saint Alphonsus de Liguori

Saint Teresa of Avila, keep me always focused on Jesus, my Lord, and protect me from the assaults of the evil one. Amen.

To Saint Catherine of Siena

More than once, Saint Catherine of Siena was physically attacked by demons because of the success her prayers and penances had in turning people back to God. She herself admitted, "The devil fears hearts on fire with love of God."

Heavenly Father, your glory is in your saints. We praise your glory in the life of the admirable Saint Catherine of Siena, virgin and doctor of the Church. Her whole life was a noble sacrifice inspired by an ardent love of Jesus, your unblemished Lamb. In troubled times she strenuously upheld the rights of his beloved spouse, the Church. Father, honor her merits and hear her prayers for each of us. Help us to pass unscathed through the corruption of this world. Help us always to see in the Vicar of Christ an anchor in the storms of life and a beacon of light to the harbor of your love, in this dark night of your times and men's souls. Grant also to each of us our special petition *(mention it here)*. We ask this through Jesus, your Son, in the bond of the Holy Spirit. Amen.

Saint Catherine of Siena, pray for us.

To Saint John Vianney

The devil tormented Saint John Vianney through loud, taunting, and harrowing voices at night, making it impossible for him to get any sleep. At first the saint was very much afraid, but once he realized that these unearthly voices were from demons, his alarm was allayed and, putting his trust in God, he learned to live with the torture—which lasted not for days or months, but for thirty-five years! He once said, "The demon is very cunning, but he is not strong. Making a Sign of the Cross soon puts him to flight."

O holy Curé of Ars, Saint John Vianney, you had a heart completely in love with Jesus and you faithfully served God by serving his people as their priest. Pray that we might have the same desire to live our lives completely for the Lord and to bring others with us as we travel to our heavenly homeland.

You encountered many obstacles and trials throughout your life and gave us the example of always staying united to Jesus in the midst of difficulty. See our fears and anxieties, our vulnerability in the face of temptation and the evils that surround us. Help us to have courage and strength in the face of difficulties or obstacles that may lead us away from God and his will for us. We ask your intercession for our particular needs and intentions (*mention request*) and we trust that you will bring them before Jesus for us.

Saint John Vianney, give us a heart like yours: a heart that loves Jesus and the gift of the sacraments. Help us to have a deep devotion to Mary our mother as you did. We ask this through Christ our Lord. Amen.

To Saint Padre Pio

In written correspondence to his spiritual director on December 20, 1910, Padre Pio wrote: "I find myself in the hands of the demon, who is struggling to tear me from the arms of Jesus. My God, what battles he stirs within me! Sometimes it is all I can do to hold on to my senses because of the constant violence I must inflict on myself. My father, how many tears and sighs I address to heaven asking to be liberated from this toil. But it does not matter; I will not tire of praying to Jesus."[7]

Devout priest of God, Saint Padre Pio, you spent countless hours in the confessional seeking to reconcile sinners to God. I come before you with deep sorrow for my sins. Help me to recognize and repent of my sins, and to be always faithful to the teachings of Jesus. Preserve me from evil and from the temptations and attacks of the devil.

Teach me to seek God in all things and pray for me, that God may not look upon my sins but upon my desire to always please him. Plead for mercy for me before God, and especially pray for the intention that I entrust to you (*mention request*).

I ask everything in the name of our Lord Jesus Christ, who lives and reigns with the Father in the unity of the Holy Spirit, one God, for ever and ever. Amen.

To Saint Gemma Galgani

Saint Gemma Galgani is noted for the mystical graces she received and for her generous and loving participation in the passion of Christ, but also for the many battles the devil waged against her. Jesus himself warned her beforehand that Satan was about to attack so that she would not be afraid or find herself unprepared. He told her, "Remain calm, because I am always in your heart."

Saint Gemma, you always showed compassionate love for those in distress, and had a great desire to help them. Help me also in my present needs and obtain for me the favor I humbly implore, if it be profitable for my soul (*mention it*).

The numerous miracles and the wonderful favors attributed to your intercession instill in me the confidence that you can help me. Pray to Jesus, your Spouse, for me. Show him the stigmata which his love has given you. Remind him of the blood that flowed from these same wounds, the excruciating pain you suffered, the tears you shed for the salvation of souls. Place all this as your precious treasure in a chalice of love, and Jesus will hear you. Amen.

To Saint Veronica Giuliani

Saint Veronica Giuliani is a Capuchin saint. She served as novice mistress and then as abbess in her community in her monastery in Città di Costello, Italy. She was both a practical person and a mystic, who lived everything in union with Christ and for love of him. Jesus rewarded her by transferring the crown of thorns from his head to hers.

During her religious life, she was frequently plagued by Satan, who would push her down the stairs, beat her, and throw bricks at her, because he was so upset with her prayers and penances for sinners.

O God, who declare that you abide in hearts that are pure, grant that through the intercession of the virgin Saint Veronica Giuliani we may be so fashioned by your grace that we become a dwelling pleasing to you.

Saint Veronica, teach us to love God, to follow his will in all things, united to him in love and a sacramental life. In this way, evil will have no power over us. May we draw strength from the passion and death of our Lord Jesus Christ, who lives and reigns with the Father in the unity of the Holy Spirit, one God, for ever and ever. Amen.

To Blessed Bartolo Longo

Blessed Bartolo Longo had a long journey back to God. After his mother died when he was ten, he lost his way in the confusion of the world and as a young man he became a Satanist priest and promised his soul to the devil. A professor from the university in Naples that Bartolo attended was successful in convincing him to see a Dominican priest, who eventually won him back into the Church and gave him absolution. Bartolo became a zealous and holy apostle of the Rosary, spending himself for the salvation of others.

O Blessed Bartolo Longo, you loved Mary our mother with the love of a son and spread devotion to her Rosary everywhere you went. Through her you learned to trust in the mercy and forgiveness of God, and from her you learned to serve Christ in his suffering brothers and sisters. Teach me to live in a spirit of prayer united to God, to never doubt his mercy or forgiveness, and to nurture a tender devotion to Mary and to her Rosary. You preached that whoever prayed the Rosary would never be lost. Grant me a deep love for this powerful Gospel prayer and let it be a means of always drawing me closer to Jesus. I trust in the intercession of his Mother and in your prayers for me to lead a life holy and pleasing to God. I ask all this through our Lord Jesus Christ, who lives and reigns with the Father in the unity of the Holy Spirit, one God, for ever and ever. Amen.

Prayer to My Patron Saint for Protection

Heavenly Father, through the intercession of [*mention your patron saint*] I ask you to guard me against every danger of soul and body. Deliver me from every evil and direct me along the path of holiness, until the day I am united with you and all the saints in heaven. Amen.

Litany of the Saints

The Litany of the Saints is another proven powerful prayer of protection; all the saints of heaven are eager to come to our aid in the war against evil. When praying the litany privately, you might also want to add your own patron saint or your favorite saints, invoking their intercession for your needs.

Lord, *have mercy on us.*

Christ, *have mercy on us.*

Lord, *have mercy on us.*

Christ, *hear us.*

Christ, *graciously hear us.*

   Response: have mercy on us

God, the Father of heaven, *R.*

God the Son, Redeemer of the world, *R.*

God the Holy Spirit, *R.*

Holy Trinity, one God, *R.*

Response: pray for us

Holy Mary, *R.*

Holy Mother of God, *R.*

Holy Virgin of virgins, *R.*

Saint Michael, *R.*

Saint Gabriel, *R.*

Saint Raphael, *R.*

All you holy angels and archangels, *R.*

All you holy orders of blessed spirits, *R.*

Saint John the Baptist, *R.*

Saint Joseph, *R.*

All you holy patriarchs and prophets, *R.*

Saint Peter, *R.*

Saint Paul, *R.*

Saint Andrew, *R.*

Saint James the Greater, *R.*

Saint John, *R.*

Saint Thomas, *R.*

Saint James the Lesser, *R.*

Saint Philip, *R.*

Saint Bartholomew, *R.*

Saint Matthew, *R.*

Saint Simon, *R.*

Saint Thaddeus, *R.*

Saint Matthias, *R.*

Saint Barnabas, *R.*

Saint Luke, *R.*

Saint Mark, *R.*

All you holy apostles and evangelists, *R.*

All you holy disciples of the Lord, *R.*

All you holy innocents, *R.*

Saint Stephen, *R.*

Saint Lawrence, *R.*

Saint Vincent, *R.*

Saints Fabian and Sebastian, *R.*

Saints John and Paul, *R.*

Saints Cosmas and Damian, *R.*

Saints Gervase and Protase, *R.*

All you holy martyrs, *R.*

Saint Sylvester, *R.*

Saint Gregory, *R.*

Saint Ambrose, *R.*

Saint Augustine, *R.*

Saint Jerome, *R.*

Saint Martin, *R.*

Saint Nicholas, *R.*

All you holy bishops and confessors, *R.*

All you holy doctors, *R.*

Saint Anthony, *R.*

Saint Benedict, *R.*

Saint Bernard, *R.*

Saint Dominic, *R.*

Saint Francis, *R.*

All you holy priests and friars, *R.*

All you holy monks and hermits, *R.*

Saint Mary Magdalene, *R.*

Saint Agatha, *R.*

Saint Lucy, *R.*

Saint Agnes, *R.*

Saint Cecilia, *R.*

Saint Catherine, *R.*

Saint Anastasia, *R.*

Saint Clare, *R.*

All you holy virgins and widows, *R.*

All you holy men and women, saints of God,
  intercede for us.

Be merciful, *spare us, O Lord.*

Be merciful, *graciously hear us, O Lord.*

  Response: *Lord, deliver us.*

From all evil, *R.*

From all sin, *R.*

From sudden and violent death, *R.*

From the snares of the devil, *R.*

From hatred and hostility, *R.*

From natural disasters, *R.*

From earthquakes and hurricanes, *R.*

From sickness, famine, and war, *R.*

From everlasting death, *R.*

By the mystery of your Incarnation, *R.*

By your birth, *R.*

By your baptism and holy fasting, *R.*

By your cross and passion, *R.*

By your death and burial, *R.*

By your holy resurrection, *R.*

By your admirable ascension, *R.*

By the coming of the Holy Spirit,
　　the Paraclete, *R.*

In the day of judgment, *R.*

　Response: *we beseech you, hear us.*

Although we are sinners, *R.*

That you pardon us, *R.*

That you bring us to true repentance, *R.*

That you govern and guard your holy
　　Church, *R.*

That you watch over the Pope and bishops, *R.*

That you grant peace and true harmony among
　　nations, *R.*

That you deign to provide and preserve the
　　fruits of the earth, *R.*

That you grant peace and unity to all
　　Christians, *R.*

That you confirm and preserve us in your holy
　　service, *R.*

That you lift our minds and hearts to heavenly
　　desires, *R.*

That you grant eternal blessings to all our bene-
factors, *R.*

That you grant eternal blessings to all our
family members, relatives, and loved ones, *R.*

That you grant eternal rest to all the faithful
departed, *R.*

Jesus Christ, Son of God, *R.*

Lamb of God, you take away the sins of the
world, *spare us, O Lord.*

Lamb of God, you take away the sins of the
world, *graciously hear us, O Lord.*

Lamb of God, you take away the sins of the
world, *have mercy on us.*

Let us pray.

Almighty, everlasting God, hear the prayers
of your Church, and in your mercy grant our
petitions, through your Son, our Lord Jesus
Christ, who lives and reigns with you in the
unity of the Holy Spirit, one God forever and
ever. Amen.

X

Spiritual Warfare Prayers

The prayers in this section are taken from the long-standing treasury of the Church's tradition for use by the laity. They are prayers to be used for one's self or for those one has authority over (e.g., parents for their children and children for their parents, or spouses for one another). They are especially recommended in times of temptation.

Sealing Prayer of Protection

The person seals himself with Holy Oil:[*]

I ask Jesus to seal me in his most Precious Blood against any and all incursions of the evil one, in particular against any clinging, familial, familiar, or retaliating spirits, ✠ in the name of the Father and of the Son and of the Holy Spirit. Amen.

---

[*] This Holy Oil is any type of olive oil blessed by a priest; it is primarily used for healing and protection against harm and can be used in praying for oneself or for others. It is not to be confused with one of the three Sacred Oils used in the sacraments. To seal yourself, simply make a cross with blessed oil on your forehead.

Prayer of Command

In his name and by the power of his cross and Blood, I ask Jesus to bind any evil spirits, forces and powers of the earth, air, fire, or water, of the netherworld and the satanic forces of nature. By the power of the Holy Spirit and by his authority, I ask Jesus Christ to break any curses, hexes, or spells and send them back to where they came from, if it be his holy will. I beseech you, Lord Jesus, to protect us by pouring your Precious Blood on us (my family, etc.), which you have shed for us, and I ask you to command that any departing spirits leave quietly, without disturbance, and go straight to Jesus Christ for him to dispose of as he sees fit. I ask you to bind any demonic interaction, interplay, or communications. I place (*name*: person, place, or thing) under the protection of the Blood of Jesus Christ which he shed for us. Amen.

Carmelite Invocation

Come, Holy Spirit, with your seven-fold gifts, and anoint us with your divine light, wisdom, and power. Come, Lord Jesus Christ, and anoint us with your Precious Blood, freeing us from every snare and stronghold of the principalities and powers of darkness. O Mother of God, glorious and Immaculate and ever Virgin Mary, come and crush the head of the ancient serpent. O great father Saint Joseph, terror of demons, come and annihilate the enemies of our souls. Saint Michael, great prince and commander of the heavenly army, strike down the insidious foes who seek to destroy us. Come glorious band of apostles, come great patriarchs and prophets; come white-robed army of martyrs, come pure and noble throng of virgins. Come to our aid holy mother Saint Teresa, our holy father Saint John of the Cross, Saint Elijah, Saint Elisha, Saint John the Baptist, Saint Therese, all you saints of Carmel, Saint Pio, Saint Isaac Jogues and companions, Saint Faustina, Saint Benedict, Saint Francis, Saint Anthony, Saint Clare, our guardian angels, archangels, and all you holy angels and saints; come repulse the attacks and deceits of our wicked enemies; render them impotent and helpless. Let God arise; let his enemies be scattered, and all those who hate him flee before him. As smoke is driven away, so are they driven away; as wax melts before the fire, so the wicked perish at the presence of God.

Invocation of the Entire Heavenly Court

O Glorious Queen of Heaven and earth, Virgin Most Powerful, you who have the power to crush the head of the ancient serpent with your heel, come and exercise this power flowing from the grace of your Immaculate Conception. Shield us under the mantle of your purity and love, draw us into the sweet abode of your heart, and annihilate and render impotent the forces bent on destroying us. Come Most Sovereign Mistress of the Holy Angels and Mistress of the Most Holy Rosary, you who from the very beginning have received from God the power and the mission to crush the head of Satan. We humbly beseech you, send forth your holy legions, that under your command and by your power they may pursue the evil spirits, encounter them on every side, resist their bold attacks, and drive them far from us, harming no one on the way, binding them immobile to the foot of the cross to be judged and sentenced by Jesus Christ your Son and to be disposed of by him as he wills. Saint Joseph, Patron of the Universal Church, come to our aid in this grave battle against the forces of darkness, repel the attacks of the devil and free your son/daughter (*name*), from the strong hold the enemy has upon his/her soul. Saint Michael, summon the entire heavenly court to engage their forces in this fierce battle against the powers of hell. Come O Prince of Heaven with your mighty sword and thrust into hell Satan and all the other evil spirits. O guardian angels, guide and protect us. Amen.

Breastplate of Saint Patrick

I arise today
Through a mighty strength, the invocation
   of the Trinity,
Through belief in the Threeness,
Through confession of the Oneness
of the Creator of creation.

I arise today
Through the strength of Christ's birth
  with his baptism,
Through the strength of his crucifixion with
  his burial,
Through the strength of his resurrection
  with his ascension,
Through the strength of his descent for
  the judgment of doom.

I arise today
Through the strength of the love of
  cherubim,
In the obedience of angels,
In the service of archangels,
In the hope of resurrection to meet
  with reward,
In the prayers of patriarchs,
In the predictions of prophets,
In the preaching of apostles,
In the faith of confessors,
In the innocence of holy virgins,
In the deeds of righteous men.

I arise today, through
The strength of heaven,

The light of the sun,
The radiance of the moon,
The splendor of fire,
The speed of lightning,
The swiftness of wind,
The depth of the sea,
The stability of the earth,
The firmness of rock.

I arise today, through
God's strength to pilot me,
God's might to uphold me,
God's wisdom to guide me,
God's eye to look before me,
God's ear to hear me,
God's word to speak for me,
God's hand to guard me,
God's shield to protect me,
God's host to save me
From snares of devils,
From temptation of vices,
From everyone who shall wish me ill,
afar and near.

I summon today
All these powers between me and those evils,

Against every cruel and merciless power
that may oppose my body and soul,
Against incantations of false prophets,
Against black laws of pagandom,
Against false laws of heretics,
Against craft of idolatry,
Against spells of witches and smiths and
    wizards,
Against every knowledge that corrupts man's
    body and soul;
Christ to shield me today
Against poison, against burning,
Against drowning, against wounding,
So that there may come to me an abundance
    of reward.
Christ with me,
Christ before me,
Christ behind me,
Christ in me,
Christ beneath me,
Christ above me,
Christ on my right,
Christ on my left,
Christ when I lie down,

Christ when I sit down,
Christ when I arise,
Christ in the heart of every man who
    thinks of me,
Christ in the mouth of everyone who
    speaks of me,
Christ in every eye that sees me,
Christ in every ear that hears me.

I arise today
Through a mighty strength, the invocation
    of the Trinity,
Through belief in the Threeness,
Through confession of the Oneness
of the Creator of creation.

Prayer of Authority

Lord Jesus Christ, in your name, I ask you to
bind and silence all powers and forces that do
not accept you as Lord and King, in the air, in
the water, in the ground, the netherworld and
nature and the spiritual world. I ask you to bind
all demonic action and demonic communica-
tion. Lord, seal this whole place, all of us here,

and all our intentions in the Precious Blood of Jesus Christ. Mary, we ask you to surround us with your mantle of protection and crush Satan's power in our lives. Saint Michael the Archangel, we ask you and all our guardian angels to defend us in battle against Satan and the powers of darkness. Amen.

Binding Prayer

Jesus Christ, our Lord and God, I ask you to render all spirits impotent, paralyzed, and ineffective in attempting to take revenge against any one of us, our families, friends, communities, those who pray for us and their family members, or anyone associated with us. I ask you to bind and sever and cut off all evil spirits, all powers in the air, the water, the ground, the fire, the underground, the netherworld, any satanic forces in nature and any and all emissaries of the satanic headquarters. I ask you to bind in your blood all of their attributes, aspects, and characteristics, all of their interactions, communications, and deceitful games. I break any and all bonds, ties, and attachments ✠ in the name of the Father and of the Son and of the Holy Spirit. Amen.

Another form:

Jesus, I ask you to bind and seal all power sources attached to either/any of us in your Most Precious Blood, and I ask you to render them all completely helpless, impotent, neutralized, paralyzed, and ineffective, ✠ in the name of the Father and of the Son and of the Holy Spirit. Amen. (*Thrice*).

Prayer of Purification

Lord Jesus Christ, we pray that you cover us, our families, and all of our possessions with your love and your Most Precious Blood, and surround all of us with your heavenly angels, saints, and the mantle of our Blessed Mother. Thank you, Lord, Jesus Christ. We ask this in your most holy name.

Act of Rejection and Consecration

I reject any dedication, consecration, vow, pact, promise, contract or blood contract, covenant or blood covenant to Satan of myself (*and insert names of others if you have made generational consecrations or included anyone else when making an offering to Satan*), my heart, spirit, soul, body, mind, memory, imagination, intellect, will, dreams, inner thoughts, subliminal thoughts, touch, taste, smell, sight, hearing, stomach, blood, healthy bacteria, immune system, nervous system, and all other internal processes, especially through (*insert list of names . . .*) ✢ in the name of the Father and of the Son and of the Holy Spirit. Amen. (*Thrice*)

I consecrate myself and my heart, spirit, soul, body, mind, memory, imagination, intellect, will, dreams, inner thoughts, subliminal thoughts, touch, taste, smell, sight, hearing, stomach, blood, healthy bacteria, immune system, nervous system, and all other internal processes, to the Sacred Heart of Jesus and the Immaculate Heart of Mary, ✢ in the name of the Father and of the Son and of the Holy Spirit. Amen.

Prayer for Protection Against Curses, Harm, and Accidents

Lord Jesus, I ask you to protect our family from sickness, from all harm, and from accidents. If any of us has been subjected to any curses, hexes, or spells, I beg you to declare these curses, hexes, or spells null and void. If any evil spirits have been sent against us, I ask Christ to decommission you, and I ask that you be sent to the foot of his cross to be dealt with as he will. Then, Lord, I ask you to send your holy angels to guard and protect all of us.

Prayers for Breaking Curses of the Occult

I ask Jesus to bind in his Most Precious Blood any and all evil curses, pacts, spells, seals, hexes, vexes, triggers, trances, vows, demonic blessings, or any other demonic bondages sent against (*name*) or myself, or any of our loved ones or any of our possessions; I ask him to bind them all and break them. ✟ In the name of the Father and of the Son and of the Holy Spirit. (*Thrice*)

Prayer Against Every Evil

Almighty God—Father, Son, and Holy Spirit, Most Holy Trinity—Immaculate Virgin Mary, all angels, archangels, and saints of heaven, descend upon me. Please purify me, Lord, mold me, fill me with yourself, and use me. Banish all the forces of evil from me, destroy them, vanquish them, so that I do your holy will. Banish from me all spells, witchcraft, black magic, malefice, ties, maledictions, and the evil eye; diabolic infestations, oppressions, possessions; all that is evil and sinful; jealousy, perfidy, envy; physical, psychological, moral, spiritual, diabolical ailments. Cast into hell all demons working these evils, that they may never again touch me or any other creature in the entire world. I command and bid all the powers who molest me by the power of God Almighty, in the name of Jesus Christ our Savior, through the intercession of the Immaculate Virgin Mary, to leave me forever, and to be consigned into the everlasting hell.

Prayer of Deliverance

Almighty God and Father, we beg you through the intercession and help of the Archangels, Saints Michael, Raphael, and Gabriel, for the deliverance of our brothers and sisters who are enslaved by the evil one. All you saints of heaven come to our aid.

From anxiety, sadness, and obsessions,
we implore you, deliver us, O Lord.
From hatred, fornication, and envy,
we implore you, deliver us, O Lord.
From thoughts of jealousy, rage, and death,
we implore you, deliver us, O Lord.
From every thought of suicide and abortion,
we implore you, deliver us, O Lord.
From every form of sinful sexuality,
we implore you, deliver us, O Lord.
From every division in our family, and every harmful friendship,
we implore you, deliver us, O Lord.
From every sort of spell, malefice, witchcraft, and every form of the occult,
we implore you, deliver us, O Lord.

You who said, "Peace I leave with you, my peace I give to you," grant that, through the intercession of the Virgin Mary, we may be liberated from every demonic influence and enjoy your peace always. In the name of Christ, our Lord. Amen.

Prayer to Overcome Evil Passions and to Become a Saint

Dear Jesus, in the Sacrament of the Altar, be forever thanked and praised. Love, worthy of all celestial and terrestrial love! Out of infinite love for me, an ungrateful sinner, you did assume our human nature, did shed your Most Precious Blood in the cruel scourging, and did expire on a shameful cross for our eternal welfare! Now, illumined with lively faith, with the outpouring of my whole soul and the fervor of my heart, I humbly beseech you, through the infinite merits of your painful sufferings, to give me strength and courage to destroy every evil passion which sways my heart, to bless you in my greatest afflictions, to glorify you by the exact fulfilment of my duties, supremely to hate all sin, and thus to become a saint.

Prayer Against Retaliation

Lord Jesus Christ, in your love and mercy, pour your Precious Blood over me so that no demon or disembodied spirit may retaliate against me. Mary, surround me with your mantle, blocking any retaliating spirits from having any authority over me. Saint Michael, surround me with your shield, so that no evil spirit may take revenge on me. Queen of Heaven and Saint Michael, send down the legions of angels under your command to fight off any spirits that would seek to harm me. All you saints of heaven impede any retaliating spirit from influencing me. Lord, you are the just Judge, the avenger of the wicked, the Advocate of the just; we beg you, in your mercy, that all we ask of Mary, the angels, and the saints of heaven be also granted to all our loved ones, those who pray for us and their loved ones, that for your glory's sake, we may enjoy your perfect protection. Amen.

Short-Form Deliverance

In the name of the Lord Jesus Christ, by the power of his cross, his Blood and his resurrection, I bind you Satan, the spirits, powers and forces of darkness, the nether world, and the evil forces of nature. I take authority over all curses, hexes, demonic activity, and spells directed against me, my relationships, ministry, air space, finances, and the work of my hands; and I break them by the power and authority of our Lord Jesus Christ. I bind all demonic interaction, interplay, and communications between spirits sent against me, and send them directly to Jesus Christ for him to deal with as he wills. I ask forgiveness for and denounce all negative inner vows that I have made with the enemy, and ask that Jesus Christ release me from these vows and from any bondage they may have held in me. I claim the shed Blood of Jesus Christ, the Son of the living God, over every aspect of my life for my protection. I pray all these things in the precious name of my Lord and Savior, Jesus Christ.

Perimeter Prayer

A. I adjure all you evil spirits, in the name of the spotless Lamb of God, Jesus of Nazareth, to depart from here. I cast you out, every unclean spirit, every phantom, every encroachment of the devil. Yield then to God! You are vanquished in your citadel, all you vile demons. The most Sovereign Queen of Heaven, the glorious and ever Virgin Mary, through her immaculate purity drives you out; before her countenance you must flee. Give way, you evil spirits, to the Queen of Heaven. She is destined by almighty God to crush your head with her heel.

B. Lord Jesus Christ, in your love and mercy establish a perimeter of protection around (*name*) and myself, and all our loved ones, those who pray for us and their loved ones. May the holy angels guard him/her/us and all our possessions, establishing a perimeter of protection around (*name*), rendering him/her/us immune from any kind of demonic influence. I ask that no demonic bondage, door, portron,[*] demonic entity, portal, astral projection, or disembodied spirit may enter the space of one hundred yards in all directions of him/her/us. I ask that any demons within this vicinity or any that should try to enter here be rendered deaf, dumb, and blind; that you strip them of all weapons, armor, power, illusions, and authority; that you bind, rebuke, and disable them from communicating or interacting with each other in any way. Remove them, sending them directly to the foot of your cross. Jesus, Son of the Most High, I ask this in your glorious and most holy name. Amen.

Spiritual Warfare Prayer

Heavenly Father, I love you, I praise you, and I worship you. I thank you for sending your Son Jesus who won victory over sin and death for my salvation. I thank you for sending your Holy

---

*A portron is a demon who stands guard at a portal.

Spirit who strengthens me, guides me, and leads me into fullness of life. I thank you for Mary, my heavenly mother, who intercedes, with the holy angels and saints, for me.

Lord Jesus Christ, I place myself at the foot of your cross and ask you to cover me with your Precious Blood, which pours forth from your Most Sacred Heart and your Most Holy Wounds. Purify me, O Lord, in the living water that flows from your Heart. I ask you to surround me, Lord Jesus, with your holy light.

Heavenly Father, let your healing grace flow through the maternal and paternal generations to purify my family line of Satan and sin. I come before you, Father, and ask forgiveness for myself, my relatives, and my ancestors, for any calling upon powers that set themselves up in opposition to you or that do not offer true honor to Jesus Christ. In the most holy name of Jesus, I now reclaim any territory that was handed over to Satan and place it under the lordship of Jesus Christ.

By the power of your Holy Spirit, reveal to me, Father, any people I need to forgive and any areas of unconfessed sin. Reveal aspects of my life that are not pleasing to you, O Father, and ways that have given or could give Satan a foothold in my life. Father, I submit to you any unforgiveness; I submit to you my sins; and I submit to you all of the ways that Satan has a hold on my life. Thank you, O Father for this knowledge; thank you, for your forgiveness and your love.

Lord Jesus, in your holy name, I bind all evil spirits of the air, water, ground, underground, and netherworld. I further bind, in the name of Jesus, any and all emissaries of the satanic headquarters and claim the Precious Blood of Jesus on the air, atmosphere, water, ground and their fruits around us, the underground, and the netherworld.

Heavenly Father, allow your Son Jesus to come now with the Holy Spirit, the Blessed Virgin Mary, the holy angels, and the saints to protect me from all harm and to keep all evil spirits from taking revenge on me in any way.

Lord Jesus Christ, fill me with charity, compassion, faith, gentleness, hope, humility, joy, kindness, light, love, mercy, modesty, patience, peace, purity, security, serenity, tranquility, trust, truth, understanding, and wisdom. Help me to walk in your light and truth, illuminated by the Holy Spirit so that I may praise, honor, and glorify our Father in time and in eternity. For you, Lord Jesus, are the Way, the Truth, and the Life, and you have come that we might have life and have it more abundantly.

Prayer Against Evil

Based on Psalm 68, this prayer can be prayed by itself or as a chaplet using rosary beads. If prayed as a chaplet, the Saint Michael prayer (p. 100) is said on the Our Father beads of a rosary; then the following prayer is said ten times on the Hail Mary beads:

Let God arise, let his enemies be scattered, and let those who hate him flee before his face. May they vanish like smoke and melt like wax before the presence of the Lord.

Invocations for Deliverance

O Blood and Water, which poured forth from the Heart of Jesus as a fount of mercy for us, I trust in you.

O my God, free me from every evil of mind, heart, spirit, and body, that I may enjoy your peace always, in the name of Jesus Christ, our Lord. Amen.

Notes

1. *A Select Library of the Nicene and Post-Nicene Fathers of the Christian Church: St. Chrysostom: On the priesthood; Ascetic treatises; Select homilies and letters; Homilies on the statutes*, ed. Philip Schaff (New York: Charles Scribner's Sons, 1903), 9:171.

2. See Pope Francis, "Holy Mass on the Feast of the Translation of the Miraculous Image of Our Lady *Salus Populi Romani*" (Homily of His Holiness Pope Francis, Basilica of Saint Mary Major, January 28, 2018), http://www.vatican.va/content/francesco/en/homilies/2018/documents/papa-francesco_20180128_omelia-traslazione-icona.html.

3. Gabriele Amorth, SSP, *An Exorcist: More Stories*, trans. Nicoletta V. MacKenzie (San Francisco: Ignatius Press, 2002), 199.

4. Author translation from the Italian, "Eco di Maria Regina della Pace," Vol. 168, Marzo-Aprile, 2003, https://www.medjugorje.ws/it/echo/echo-168/

5. See Teresa of Avila, *The life of St. Teresa of Jesus, of the Order of Our Lady of Carmel*, trans. David Lewis (London: T. Baker, 1916), 288.

6. Ibid., 284.

7. *Secrets of a Soul: Padre Pio's Letters to His Spiritual Directors*, ed. Gianluigi Pasquale (Boston: Pauline Books & Media, 2003), 19.

List of Contributors

All prayers were taken from common sources, with the exception of those credited in the text and the following:

Gabriele Amorth, SSP
To Our Lord Jesus   61

Msgr. G. Bardi
To Saint Gemma Galgani   122

Julia Mary Darrenkamp, FSP
Prayer for the Fruits of the Holy Spirit   68

Brian Moore, SJ
Prayer to the Holy Spirit   67

Marianne Lorraine Trouvé, FSP
Prayer Against Evil   157

Mary Leonora Wilson, FSP
To Saint Mary Magdalene   114

Special Bulk Prices Available!*

Get multiple copies of *Essential Healing Prayers for Peace and Strength* and *Essential Spiritual Warfare Prayers for Protection and Deliverance* for gifts, parish groups, RCIA candidates and catechumens, friends, and family.

    20 + for $6 each
    50 + for $5 each
    100 + for $4 each

For U.S. bulk orders, online ordering available at https://paulinestore.com/spiritual-warfare-prayers or visit your local Pauline Books & Media book store.

For Canadian bulk orders, online ordering available at https://paulinestore.ca/spiritual-warfare-prayers or visit our Pauline Books & Media book store in Toronto.

*Prices subject to change. Bulk offer for trade and wholesale customers is net.